Helen Mathers

**Eyre's acquittal:**

A sequel to 'Story of a sin' - Vol. 3

Helen Mathers

**Eyre's acquittal:**
*A sequel to 'Story of a sin' - Vol. 3*

ISBN/EAN: 9783337821265

Printed in Europe, USA, Canada, Australia, Japan

Cover: Foto ©ninafisch / pixelio.de

More available books at **www.hansebooks.com**

# EYRE'S ACQUITTAL.

*A SEQUEL TO*
'STORY OF A SIN.'

BY
HELEN MATHERS,
AUTHOR OF 'COMIN' THRO' THE RYE,' ETC.

IN THREE VOLUMES.
VOL. III.

LONDON:
RICHARD BENTLEY AND SON,
Publishers in Ordinary to Her Majesty the Queen.
1884.

*[All Rights Reserved.]*

*'I had happier died by thee
   Than lived on as Lady Leigh.'*

# EYRE'S ACQUITTAL.

*BOOK III.—continued.*

## CHAPTER VI.

*'Nature never did betray the heart that loved her.'*

COME with me on tiptoe beneath the trees that poor Wolsey planted for the ultimate benefit of a thankless king, till we are close to the ha-ha that divides us from a meadow more glorious with its buttercups than was ever cloth-of-gold; turn your back on the red-brick house that blinks beyond in the sunshine, then choose the trunk that shall best afford you its lusty support, and look around you.

Coolness, space, and light are here; light, that falls in glory only to be broken into trembling patches by the quick dance of the shadow-leaves reflected from above; space, that seems to know no limit as your eye sweeps the perspective of green aisles to right and left; and coolness so pure and deep as to soothe the senses like a charm, and breathe into them a mere physical sense of rest that is in itself an exquisite joy.

Out yonder the world goes by, yet so far away that its echo hardly reaches you .... and between you and it lies a carpet of white and red, flung royally down by the chestnuts as their proud beauty waned .... nearer yet, in a golden slant of sunshine, falls a shower of green rain, only no rain ever dropped half so coyly, so beautifully, or wore so fine a tint, for these are the scatterings from the blossomed limes overhead, breathing sweetness as they fall, and adding the one touch that crowns and makes perfect this most perfect hour and scene.

Sound there is none, save the faint low murmur given out by the boughs, and that vaguely resembles the far-off sob of ocean (but the ear must be keen that will hear it), and the distant note of a cuckoo who lives in the grove yonder, and who is heard year after year, and far into the spring, long after cuckoo-flowers have come and gone, and the anemones with which his retreat is speckled.

'This is heaven,' says a girl's voice, breaking the stillness; but the voice is so sweet that no note of discord with the scene is sounded.

'No, it is not heaven, but it is peace,'

answers another voice, in which no peace is, but a curious yearning, as though an unsatisfied heart speaks in it, and something more than peace is needed to content her.

'Has anyone vexed you?' says the first voice gently.

'No one. Yet I am restless—out of sorts. This very silence frets me, and I am no happier here than if I had stayed at home.'

'Are you anxious about your father?'

'Not more than usual.'

'Then your trouble is in your own heart. Why do you look sad even in the midst of your brightest triumphs, and when even envy cannot discover a flaw in your lot?'

'Am I so triumphant?' said the other voice. 'Listen. It was a custom among the Romans, on the occasion of a great victory, to appoint three especial honours to the victor. The first honour, that the people should meet the conqueror with acclamations and every other testimony of pleasure; the second, that all the captives, bound hand and foot, should attend the victor's chariot; the third honour, that, enwrapped in the mantle of Jupiter, he should sit upon a triumphal car, drawn by four white horses, and be thus brought to the capitol. But lest these exalted rewards should swell the heart, and make the favourite of fortune forget his birth and mortal character, three grievances were attached to them. First, a slave sat on his right hand in the chariot, which served to hint that poverty and unmerited degradation were no bars to the subsequent attainment of the highest dignities. The second grievance was, that the slave should inflict upon him several severe blows to abate the haughtiness which the applause of his countrymen might tend to excite, at the same time saying to him in Greek: "Know thyself! and permit not thy exaltation to make thee proud. Look behind thee, and remember that thou art mortal." The third grievance was this, that free license was given upon that day of triumph to utter the most galling reproaches and the most cutting sarcasms.'

The voice ceased; there was a pause before the other said:

'And what are your three humiliations?'

'I have not three, but one'

'Will you tell it me?'

'No.'

'But I will guess, even though you be angry. You do not love Gordon because you love some one else.'

'Would that be an occasion for humiliation?'

'Yes, if—if——'

'He did not love me? You are right. Well, he does not love me, and I do not love him; the idea is impossible. A child may have a strong affection for a—a man, but that is not love.'

'You are not a child now.'

'I am still a child to him, for he never thought of me as any other.'

'Do you see him often?'

'I see him never.'

'You have not seen him once since you were a child?'

'Once.'

'You will see him again?'

'I do not know. That is part of my humiliation—that he could see me to-day, to-morrow, and every day, if he so willed.'

'And were you *quite* a child?'

'I was fifteen.'

'Then you were a woman. And perhaps . . . perhaps he loves you too.'

'And now that you know this, and I brought you here purposely to tell you—perhaps you will be kind to Gordon—you will marry him, and you will be happy.'

'And Gordon—will he be happy too?'

'You love him; you cannot help making him happy in the end.'

A soft ripple of laughter blended with, rather than silenced, the pause that followed; then two young faces turned, and—the one pale, the other rosy-red—looked at each other.

'Nanciebel, you have deceived me. It is not Gordon after all.'

'Yes—it is not Gordon.'

'Who is it, then?'

'Our confidences would be unequal. Tell me first of *him*.'

'He is a myth—a delusion. The ghost of something I worshipped from the time I was old enough to understand . . . and after all, I believe this fancy to be not love, but pure *memory*, and that I should find his charm gone if I saw him often in the flesh. And you—have you too such memories of *him*?'

'His presence is sweeter to me than any memory of him could be.'

'So you see him—and yet I have never surprised a sign of love in you for anyone but Gordon. Will you marry him ?'

'If he asks me.'

'You blush—yet your voice is steady, your eyes are fearless. You have nothing to fear because—he loves you.'

In the silence that followed, one of the girls turned her head aside, but the answer had been mutely given.

The voices ceased. There had not been a single note of passion in the duologue; nature had not been outraged by a single false or jarring note; softly the young maidens' love-confidences had sunk into the peace around, and made it human.

## CHAPTER VII.

'*A pious man doubting Providence, the spirit of the rose thus addressed him: "Do I not animate a beautiful plant . . . and where do you find me? Amongst thorns. But they do not sting me; they protect and give me sap. This thine enemies do for thee: and should not thy spirit be firmer than that of a frail flower?"*'

UT yonder the world and his wife scurry, skip, and amble by, never pausing to cast a look to right or left, nor dream of pausing to turn aside and explore the shade and coolness of these fragrant alleys and silent glades: all are bent on reaching the end of the avenue, and pursuing those pleasures beyond that are so much less satisfying than those they are leaving behind.

The last of the coaches passed an hour ago, and it is the humbler holiday-makers now who fill every description of vehicle, from the barouche down to the donkey-cart, while, happiest of all, the tricyclists flash in and out, with that delightful look of ease and swiftness which comes nearer than any other exercise to the actual sensation of flying.

I do not know a prettier sight than two young lovers thus seated side by side, he in his close-fitting suit of grey, with stalwart legs well shown, and she with little feet peeping out, that do their work as deftly as his—only both must bloom with good looks, both must work loyally, and as if with but one impulse between them; and I think her frock should be white and plain, descending no lower than her ankles, and round her neck and straw hat she should wear a turquoise-blue ribbon.

Why should not such a pair go a-honeymooning some day, as they have gone a-courting all this spring, in their graceful little carriage, with the tinkle of their bell for wedding-chimes behind them? Is she not already, by the mere sharing of his toil, learning to be his *help-mate* in more senses than one? So, when I see such a blithe young pair, I wish them God-speed in my heart, and my good-wishes follow the flashing wheels as they dwindle in my sight.

Look at that old pair yonder, who once may have ridden side by side, but are now on foot. See how he hands her down the slope, more tenderly, more gently now than perchance he would have done the day he married her. He hides even the beauty of the chestnuts from her—in his wrinkled face alone she finds the highest beauty; and the look that passes between them is lovely, as arm in arm they go, tottering and leaning on each other, along the way.

Look in a woman's face for the character of her husband; in the faces of her children for her own.

A man is toiling along with his hurdy-gurdy on his back, and across its top a little child, sound asleep.

Ah! that sleeping child brings many a penny to the little ugly father, who may be a rogue and a vagabond, but who loves his child, and keeps him warm and rosy, while he himself is in tatters, and always more than half-starved.

I wonder what invisible cause has set that blue-shawled, vulgar woman in yon magnificent carriage, and placed on foot and dressed in cotton the beautiful one whose beauty is as royal as it is sweet?

I wonder what home-tyrant has brought that hopeless look of sadness into the eyes and mouth of the woman who half hides them with the handful of dog-roses over which she leans? But in her hand they will wither and close, as perhaps her heart has done under a cruel grasp... Yet if to-night she set them, howsoever faded, in a bowl of water on her window-sill, where the air and wind can beat on them all night, in the morning, lo! there will be a cluster of lovely wide-opened eyes, and on the pink and white breasts bared in wild freshness to the breeze, perchance a glistening of rain-drops, through which the leaves will shine translucent, yielding up a scent exquisite, intangible, the very spirit of the flower, that has made its dwelling *here* rather than in the heart of the proud garden rose, that stiffly closes her perfumes within her, and stifles even as she blows.

So to thee, poor soul, may chance such a miracle; so may thy bruised heart yet revive and unfold itself to the healing influence of tenderness and hope ; so, too, may thy soul become ' a cup of thanksgiving full of fragrance, and an offering of sweetest incense to the Lord.'

Here come a pair of lovers on foot ; both are shabby, and both are plain ; but the man looks a churl, and probably is one. Yet despise her not for that air of loving pride, of proprietorship in him as she struts beside him ; to her he is no churl, for he has taught her the mystery of love ; and, ignoble as he may be, through him has come to her a revelation of happiness, and so poor a cause has been as potent to transform her life, to transfigure its dull routine, as if he were beautiful as one of the gods of old. She will not forget this—no woman ever does; come what will, she remembers that he made her blank life a full one, and though he become the murmuring father of her children, and a sullen, neglectful spouse, to her he will always be the lover of her youth, and however she may come to scorn and despise him, yet the thousand links that bind her to him will never be broken. She will cling to her crooked shilling to her life's end, and strive to hide its crookedness from all eyes but her own.

Look at that little barefooted urchin, with the bright curly crown outside his scanty, brimless hat; the happiest heart here to-day, till half-an-hour ago, when he grew hungry, but begged and begged behind the carriages in vain. But see—his eyes brighten, he begins to run, flitting light as thistledown over the grass till he has reached one of the last trees next the ha-ha; and there he pauses, his blue eyes fixed on a white cloth, upon which is laid a luncheon for two young ladies—a luncheon that has been carefully catered for by six young men.

A bottle of Moët and two of soda, with a tiny one of liqueur, a lobster mayonnaise, a chicken, a tongue, a roll of white bread, a pat of butter, a dish of strawberries and another of cherries—and it is at the cherries that the boy, in spite of his hunger, is looking.

'Give him some,' says the girl who has been acting as butler, and is now regarding her arrangements with some satisfaction; 'he must be a youth of taste to prefer being under these trees to watching the crowd go by out yonder!'

'I am afraid he saw the cloth afar off,' said Nanciebel, as she emptied half the cherries into the boy's chubby hands, getting a duck of the head by way of thanks as he retreated.

'Cherries won't satisfy *me*,' said Madcap gravely, as she sat down cross-legged and began to cut bread; 'I never was so hungry in my life.'

'It was a long drive down,' said Nanciebel, attacking the chicken on her knees; 'you took Gordon a good deal out of his way by your freak. But how delighted he was to find that he had not got to take us to the Derby, after all!'

'And *we* have got the best of it,' said Madcap, pausing in her occupation to glance up at the boughs that hung all their leaves outwards like a thousand mimic flags; 'and none could wish a better day on which to be born, to be married, or to die.'

'No,' said Nanciebel, and sighed very gently as she set Madcap's plate before her.

'So you can sigh for him?' said Madcap; 'then you do not love him very much.'

'But you are hungry, and so you do not love him very much.'

'And I am thirsty, too,' said Madcap presently, when her pangs had somewhat subsided, and looking round for the nippers, that, alas! the masculine forethought, which had forgotten nothing else, had altogether omitted to furnish.

'If only we had a pair of scissors!' exclaimed both girls together, and looking at the sparkling wine, that now, unattainable, appeared absolutely indispensable to their happiness.

'We could get a corkscrew at the lodge-gates,' said Nanciebel, jumping up, 'and I'll run all the way there and back!'

'Don't,' said Madcap; 'it is too hot. Couldn't we send the infant?' she added, pointing to the urchin, who, having eaten his cherries, showed his gratitude by a lively sense of favours to come, and in readiness had seated himself at no great distance on the grass.

'They would not lend it him,' said Nancy; and was gone even as she spoke, returning in less than sixty seconds, waving a pocket corkscrew triumphantly above her head.

'Nancy!' cried Madcap, gasping with amazement, 'are you a witch, or am I dreaming? You have gone to the lodge and *come back* in less than a minute!'

'Didn't you see? Perhaps there was a tree between; but I've done an awful thing!'

'You asked some one to lend it you?' said Madcap, who was now struggling with the wire, and making those faces with which ladies usually embellish the drawing of a cork, especially when there is a chance of its smiting them on the nose. 'It's coming! take care—oh!' and she sat down (as a woman always does) when the cork flew out, and did not recover from the shock till half the amber fluid had foamed itself away.

'More properly speaking, I borrowed it,' said Nanciebel, as they sat down again with their glasses beside them; 'it was not very nice thing for a young lady to ask for, was it? He looked a little astonished!'

'It was a man?' said Madcap, a little startled. 'What would Lady Ann say? I hope it was an old one?'

'Oh, quite old! and as sober as a judge. He was marching along so sedately that I knew he was to be trusted, so I stopped and said, "Oh, sir! *could* you lend me a pocket-knife, or a corkscrew?"'

'This is both,' said Madcap, taking it in her hand; 'all that is not steel is silver. He must be of a confiding temper to trust it with you. Run back with it quick, before he repents of his guilelessness, and comes to look for it himself!'

'He lent it me for half-an-hour,' said Miss Nanciebel, with great *sang-froid*; 'he said, "It is quite at your service, and you can give it me back in half-an-hour's time, when I shall be returning this way." I dropped him a curtsey and vanished.'

'Which way did he go?'

'Towards the Court. How came you to miss seeing him? He was not a hundred yards away from you.'

'I was feeding the Arab. And now for our strawberries. Alack! those men forgot the cream, but here is the sugar.'

'Madcap!'

'Nancy!'

'I told you the corkscrew man was sedate?'

'Yes.'

'But I didn't tell you he was the handsomest man I ever saw in my life!'

'Handsomer than your — invisible lover?'

'Much. Only he is fair, and I admire— never mind what I admire!'

'I expect this handsomest man of all is a mere barber's block. I think it would have been better, after all, if you had gone to the lodge.'

'I told you I had done an awful thing,' said Nanciebel, hanging her head. 'But, indeed, I saw his sedateness first, and his beauty afterwards; and I don't believe, from the way he looked at me, that he knew whether I was a girl or a boy!'

Madcap had finished her strawberries now, and with elbow on knee, and chin in hand, looked at Nanciebel, considering.

Why does a young woman look so much more lovely in the open air, in sunshine or in shadow, than in chamber or ballroom, howsoever beautifully bedecked?

Perhaps because out of doors she is in the midst of life, movement, light; because Nature in her most sportive mood finds an echo in her grace, and sees her every magical effect outdone in the changes, quick as shadows, bright as sunbeams, that will succeed each other in a young and tenderly sensitive girl-face.

'You are lovely, Nanciebel!' said Madcap at last; 'I never knew how lovely till to-day. The man must be insensible who could look at you as if you were a boy.'

'The half-hour will be up directly,' said Nanciebel, with some alarm in her blue eyes, as she looked at her watch; 'had I not better go and wait at the exact place where I met him? If not, he might take the liberty of coming on here!'

'He has the right to claim his property,' said Madcap, sitting up very erect. 'But you need not trouble yourself about it, for *I* am going to give him back the corkscrew.'

'Oh, Madcap! Well, he will look at *you!*'

'I mean to make him. If only Lady Ann could see us! or Gordon! or Doune!'

'Would—would Doune be angry?' said Miss Nanciebel timidly, and with some of her colour flitting away.

'He would have a fit! And now for the handsomest man of all!' and she sprang up.

'But how will you know him? As you say, probably our standard of good looks differs.'

'Then you must come too. We will both hide behind a tree, and when you see him coming, you will tell me. Then I shall step forward and say, " Thank you, sir!"—that is to say, if he is not a barber's block. But I should like to give him a little fright, just to shake his sedateness.'

'What will you do?'

'Set that urchin at the head of our feast, with all the remaining eatables within reach, and forbid him to stir. We will remain in hiding after the corkscrew man comes. He will look around—see nobody—then discover our white cloth, which he will probably approach, expecting to find his property upon it. When he has finally made up his mind that you are a dishonourable person, he will walk away, and I shall run after him.'

## CHAPTER VIII.

'*He's taken off the scarlet coat
Bedecked with shinin' gold,
And has put on the horseman's coat
To keep him frae the cold.*'

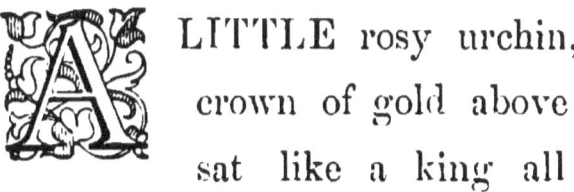 LITTLE rosy urchin, with his crown of gold above his head, sat like a king all alone at the feast spread out before him, his back to the bole of a tree, and sound asleep, with a half-eaten strawberry in his hand.

By his side leaned a partly emptied champagne bottle, out of which he had probably tasted, with instant soporific results; and beside it lay a gossamer handkerchief, in one corner of which was embroidered a somewhat uncommon name.

Out of sight, but not far away, two girls squeezed themselves closely against a trunk that would easily have hidden six; and one was impatient from waiting, and angry with herself at having lapsed into an undignified frolic, and the other was bent on playing her companion a trick.

'He has probably forgotten all about it, or he wants to punish you for accosting him, and giving him the trouble of coming back,' said Madcap indignantly; 'and any moment the coach may be in the avenue, or Lady Ann appear and find us in this ridiculous situation!'

'Look!' exclaimed Nanciebel, in a low voice, and peeping in the direction of the Court, as they had both done since they took up their station; 'don't you see a man coming—tall, and carrying himself well—and—and very well dressed?'

'So well dressed,' said Madcap drily, 'that he would look more a gentleman if he were in rags. Your handsome man is not only a barber's block, he is also a tailor's dummy! Here, take it!' and she pushed the silver corkscrew into Nanciebel's hand.

At the same moment a gentleman who had been quietly approaching from the opposite direction came to a halt before the spread cloth with a sleeping urchin at its head, and he smiled a little, as one amused; for his quick eye soon informed him that two persons, without reckoning the present ruler of the feast, had lunched there but a very short time ago.

A pair of lovers, he supposed, who were now quietly strolling in one of the distant glades, quite forgetful of his property and him? She had left some of hers behind, he thought, as he stooped and picked up the handkerchief that lay on the ground, half ashamed of his curiosity, especially as its supposed owner had created no curiosity in him whatever.

It was at this moment that Nanciebel turned and saw him, while Madcap, washing her hands of all further responsibility in the matter, quitted her hiding, and turned her face to one of the long arcades, whose end is only visible by the patch of golden sunlight that lies beyond.

The superb one was close at hand; in the background a man was staring at the corner of a girl's pocket-handkerchief, as if rooted to the spot by the fascination of the sight. Madcap's back was slowly disappearing, and Nanciebel was fain to confess that her trick had failed.

Should she call her back? She would not come; and, after all, the whole escapade was in very bad taste, and it was just as well that this stranger should suppose he had seen only one forward girl that day—not two.

But as she moved slowly towards him, she saw him turn suddenly away—only, where was the handkerchief?

There had been colour enough in her face before, but as she ran, it rose in ever warmer waves, so that she glowed like a rose when, all out of breath with haste, she at last came up with his long strides, and in a very gentle voice faltered out:

'Your corkscrew, sir!'

He turned then, looking not at, but beyond her, his right hand hidden in his breast.

'Thank you,' he said, as his roving,

eager eyes came back to her face with a look of disappointment and unwilling relief curiously blended.

How could she have called this man sedate? Nanciebel wondered. His good looks were the least part of his charm; for a splendid soul looked out of his eyes, and spoke in every expression of his features.

'And so now will you give me back the handkerchief, please?' said Nanciebel gravely.

He started and coloured.

'So you were in hiding and saw me,' he said; 'and I cannot deny the theft. But I meant you to keep what you borrowed of me in its place. My reason for stealing it was because I found on it the name—the name——'

He paused, then said abruptly:

'It is a very uncommon one; yet it appears to be yours.'

'No, it is not mine,' said Nanciebel, feeling horror at herself for extending the colloquy by a single unnecessary word. 'I never knew but one person of that name—Madcap Eyre; and the handkerchief is hers.'

'She is here to-day?' said the stranger, the blood leaping to his brow; '*here*—and with you?'

'Yes,' said Nanciebel, a little coldly; 'and now I will wish you good-afternoon, and thank you.'

She was gone before he could say another syllable, and he was left alone, standing with throbbing heart and madly-beating pulses, his hands clenched in the struggle betwixt duty and inclination that was going forward in his breast.

Through the trees he saw Nanciebel on her knees busy with packing up the plates and dishes, while the chief consumer of the feast slumbered peacefully on; and without stirring, his eager eyes roved hither and thither in search of the white flutter of a woman's gown.

How baffling were the trees! how almost hopeless a search for anyone beneath them, since you might pass within a yard of what you sought, but with the stout body of a monarch of the woods between you!

Yet desire, longing, the passionate need that cried out in him for food, however meagre, urged him with irresistible force into the way of temptation, and in another minute he was treading it with resolute, swift steps, leaving Nanciebel far behind, and fully engrossed with her task.

Madcap had wandered on, without taking

much count of time; her hat was slung on her arm, she was walking with head thrown back, and face lifted to the glories overhead, when she felt, rather than heard, a step close behind her.

'Nanciebel,' she said, 'I have had a surfeit of beauty to-day that I think will last me a long while—almost until I get back to Lovel woods.'

She got no answer, only between her gaze and the boughs through which the blue looked came a pair of eyes every whit as blue as the sky, and Madcap's charming chin came down suddenly, and all the colour went out of her cheeks as she saw who it was that stood before her.

'Madcap!' he said—'*Madcap!*' . . . the name rushing out straight from the heart, and bringing with it all the love it had gathered about it there in one tumultuous flood of joy.

So he had not forgotten her; it had been through no lack of memory that he had avoided her; and the happy colour was all back in Madcap's face, as, with her hand still in his, she looked up at him.

'You are glad to see me?' she said.

'Yes, I am glad;' but even as he spoke some of the fire died out of his eyes, as though subdued by a violent inward effort, and the vehemence of his voice suddenly sobered to one of mere affection as he let her hand go.

Somehow Madcap knew then that this moment, the full happiness of which she had not tasted, had escaped her, yet she smiled as she said:

'Are we never to meet anywhere save in a wood?'

'I spend a great deal of my time here,' he said, and with every word the change in his tone seemed to increase, and deny the passion with which he had called on her name; 'whenever I am able to leave my mother I make straight for trees, and try and fancy myself once more at Lovel.'

'Have you the late Lord Lovel's tastes as well as his features?' said Madcap, a little coldly.

'Yes; our tastes, inclinations, pursuits were identical.'

'Yet I never heard of Frank Lovel running away from, and almost hiding himself from a man whom he had condemned unheard, and to whom he refused the opportunity of explanation!' said Madcap, inwardly quaking at the effect of her words.

'And which I will refuse as long as I have breath in my body,' said Major

Methuen, with no more shame in his look and voice than if he uttered the noblest sentiments heart can applaud.

'You have some reason — some mad reason,' said Madcap, resolved to push his patience to its utmost limits, 'for your hatred of my father; but it seems that he is not singular in being the object of your aversion, for all your old friends, and all Lord Lovel's friends, you shun.'

'That is true.'

'You even shun a nearer friend—a child-friend,' said Madcap, in a low voice; 'and how can she have offended you?'

'I never had such a friend.'

'You had, for I was that friend.'

'But you were not a child; you were fifteen years old, and a woman.'

'Then you might have remembered me as a woman.'

'Have I forgotten you?'

'Entirely. It is by an accident only that you are forced to address me to-day.'

'I deliberately followed you.'

'What—from town?'

'No; I picked up your handkerchief——'

'Accident again!'

'And stole it. I was detected by a young lady who had borrowed a corkscrew——'

'What! it was *you*—and you were close to me twice over, and I never knew it?'

The girl had stopped short, her changing colour, her brilliant eyes, betraying her excitement; but in a second she had controlled it, and was walking quietly beside him.

Her words, her look, had startled him—but only for a moment. True, she remembered him kindly, fondly even, as her friend (and the heart of a young girl is tenacious of her friendships, whether for man or woman), but he was no more to her than that; and was not her engagement with Lord Lovel one of the open secrets of the town?

'Let us sit down,' said Major Methuen; and without a single backward thought of Nanciebel, of a waiting coach, or of outraged Lady Ann, Madcap leaned her back to the tree, and gave herself up to the joy of the present hour.

'Had you not an idea that chestnuts had some red in them?' she said, picking up a column of chestnut blossom that some rude hand had plucked, then cast down here to wither; 'when I was quite young, such was my fixed belief. Well, to-day I have found out my mistake. It is only when the flowers are fading that the red appears!'

'Do you remember the lecture you once read me of your country art?' he said.

'Do you?'

'Yes. Will you read me another?'

He was sitting a little behind her, but so placed that, himself unobserved, he could watch each change of her face.

'No,' she said; then added, as one thinking aloud: 'so Job died happy, after all; he *did* think you to be his "little Master Frank."'

'Who told you that?' exclaimed Major Methuen, in a startled voice.

'Was it not written on his face?' said Madcap, half looking round, 'and are you not Frank Lovel's *doppel-gänger*, and constantly mistaken for him by those who do not know that he is dead?'

'I told you that three years ago,' he said, with a chafed ring in his voice:

'that is one reason why I go abroad so seldom.'

'You could not wish to resemble a better man,' said Madcap, a little proudly; 'but the resemblance must be extraordinary, for even my father thought he recognised you as Frank.'

'And he said——' exclaimed Major Methuen, as if the words were irresistibly forced from him.

'That it was his friend's very self in the flesh; and instantly pursued you till reason convinced him of his mistake. At dinner that night we heard of the strange resemblance you bore to the late Lord Lovel, and my father resolved to see you—with the admirable results you are aware of.'

'I shall not try his patience much longer,' he said quietly. 'Mrs. Methuen is dying fast, and her death will release me from the necessity of remaining in town—or in England. Your father will scarcely think it necessary to follow me abroad.'

Was there a note of fear in his voice— a note that brought the hot colour to Madcap's cheek, and a sudden consciousness of shame that she was sitting here in friendly converse with a man who was avowedly her father's enemy? But her hottest shame was for *him*; and perhaps Major Methuen knew it as he watched the averted face, the exquisite nape of a neck that he would have given all he possessed on earth to have the right to kiss.

Suddenly she turned, and by the glow in her face, the warmth in her eye, he saw that some strong impulse was urging her to speak.

'*What* is between you?' she said. 'You

are both good—both honourable; for you are—you *must* be that, no matter how you may try to assume a shameful part. You both loved Frank: if only for that, and your likeness to him, we Eyres must' (her voice faltered) 'love you; and shall a miserable misunderstanding, that could be set to rights in five minutes of face-to-face talk, keep you away from us when we could be so—happy together?'

Gradually her voice had dwindled from the eagerness with which she began her plea to a spiritless and scarcely audible tone; for in his eyes she saw that which no words of hers could overcome, even though his heart might break beneath his stubborn will.

'Do not talk of me,' he said, 'but yourself. I watch you often, myself unseen, and I find you as unspoiled by admiration, as simple in your manners, as when I first saw you in the wood. And I do not think there is any better-hated young man in town than Gordon Lovel.'

'Why is he so well hated?' said Madcap; and from her voice one might have thought she had tears in her eyes.

'Because he is your future husband.'

There was a harsh note of envy and bitterness in the way he uttered the words that made Madcap turn, and so he saw those shining eyes that had filled indeed, but for him.

'You love him?'

As she turned her head aside, he seemed to see trembling in her all the possibilities of such a woman as God and Nature have combined to make beautiful, and keep pure . . . and was such an one to go as priceless dower to a man who might love but could never understand her? For if a woman cannot raise her husband to her own level, then she must stoop to his; and the more of happiness she brings him, the farther will she recede from the splendid promise of her youth.

'Your silence gives assent,' said Major Methuen; and none could have told from his look that in the moments when he strained heart and ear for a reply, he had lived an eternity; 'and you should be happy, for his devotion to you is one of the proverbs of the season.'

'He gives me his time.' said Madcap, who sat very cold and still, with hands tight-locked on her lap; 'and is there any surer sign than that?'

'"A man may give money because he is profuse; he may be violently fond because he is of a sanguine disposition; but if he gives me his time, he gives me an unquestionable proof of my being in full possession of his heart," or so says a great writer. And is your father satisfied with the match?' added Major Methuen abruptly.

'There is the coach!' said Madcap, starting up; 'and actually there is Lady Ann on it. They must have stopped at the Palace, and that is why Gordon is so late. Good-bye!' and without offering her hand, with only one brief glance, in which every detail of his looks stamped itself on her memory, she turned, and went swiftly away.

Where she had left him, he stood watching the beautiful young shape, the chestnut head as bright as the sunbeams that flecked it, until she had passed out of sight. Then, shifting his position, he was able to see the coach stop, and two figures in white ascend.

Did one of them turn her head and look back as the coach swept out at the lodge-gates? I am inclined to think that she did; but the man who threw himself face downwards on the grass where she had so lately sat beside him, doubted.

## CHAPTER IX.

*She wadna hae a Lowland laird,*
 *Nor be an English lady;*
*But she wad gang wi' Duncan Græme,*
 *And row her in his plaidie.'*

ONE morning in late June, Gordon read out at breakfast the announcement of Mrs. Methuen's death on the preceding day but one, and Madcap trembled; but no one looked at her, as Mr. Eyre, starting up and exclaiming, 'He cannot be out this time!' left the room, and, almost immediately after, the house.

'Poor chap! he'll be more cracked than

ever now,' said Gordon cheerfully; 'but what on earth can he mean by dodging the father these three months?'

But Madcap said nothing; only watched her opportunity to steal away to her father's study, where she sat down to restlessly await his return.

How hard the thorn of deceit pricked her heart as she sat there, and thought of the useless quest upon which her father had departed . . . why had she not said to him long ago. 'He is your enemy'? and, alas! alas! was not this the reason of her holding back the fact, that she could not add, 'and *your* enemy is *mine*'?

Not a man had attracted her heart or fancy through all the perilous chances of such a season as a fairy princess might have bestowed on her god-child; not a lover who could tempt her to lift her eyes so high as

to discover his charms or failings; for at
the root of all her coldness lay the old
reason, and '*But not like my Beverley!*'
was her unconscious thought, as, one after
another, her suitors (some for pure love's
sake, some for greed, but all seeking her
with the more zest, knowing her to be for-
bidden fruit) failed to efface an image
graven on her heart nigh on three years
ago.

Long ago she had forgiven Major
Methuen's injustice to her father, for the
root of it had been loyalty to his friend
Lord Lovel, and however Frank might
have misunderstood Mr. Eyre, he was her
hero still, and her sense of faithfulness
could appreciate even an abuse of such
partizanship; but her hope of a good
understanding between Major Methuen and
her father had dwindled and waned with

the season, and the good-bye at the cowslip-gate had come to sound in her ears like a farewell spoken from a death-bed.

At her thoughts, she covered her face with her hands, and then she sighed, because she dared not cry; and in the midst of her fears Mr. Eyre came in, his brow more dark with anger than she had ever seen it.

'The man is *out*, as usual,' he said; 'and his mother's remains are already removed to the country for burial, says the varlet who has shut the door fifty times in my face, while his master sets out for abroad immediately. But, by Heaven, I'll bring him to book before he leaves! If Frank escaped me—if others have defied me—this man *shall* not!'

But even as he spoke, he felt the impotence of the will that had so frequently failed him, and turned from Madcap with a gesture that startled her with its violence, as coming from so usually self-contained a man.

She stood quite still, looking at him, and on the very verge of confessing the one deceit she had practised towards him; and if she were betraying the faith Major Methuen had tacitly placed in her, what matter, so long as she soothed the storm in her father's breast?

But, turning suddenly, he said, 'Leave me now,' in a tone she dared not resist, and left him alone with his dark hour, his bitter thoughts, to be dressed to go to a rose-show with Lady Ann; for, as I have said, the Eyres kept very unfashionable hours.

As they turned out of Prince's Gate, a man going past in a hansom, and habited in deepest mourning, caught a glimpse of the girl's pure pale face in the white setting of her carriage, and, with a desperate resolve, turned about and followed her, though she looked at many flowers, and spoke to many people, before he got a chance of approaching her.

But as she stood behind a very tree of roses, Lady Ann being secure in the clutches of a gossip on the other side, she looked up, and saw Major Methuen standing before her.

Her heart leaped up, but her cheek was pale; her hand never dreamed of going out to his, but as they stood there face to face, the lesson that each had been learning apart, the one half-unconsciously, the other with a full knowledge of what he learned, bore its fruit, and all was over, all was said and done in the glance that they exchanged in that moment.

'I am going away for ever,' he said, and, harsh as his voice was through pain, it sounded sweet as music in her ears; 'I have only one more farewell to make: and so, for the last time, good-bye.'

'Must you go?' she said, with pale lips. 'My father is ignorant of wrong against you; for his sake—for mine—stay.'

If there was a moment's pause that seemed an eternity; if there was time for the scent and hue of the roses by which they stood to sink deep into their souls, there might have seemed none to the onlookers; but Madcap felt, rather than heard, the deep breath he drew as he said:

'I cannot—and so good-bye.'

Once he had been able to kiss her hand at parting; but now, with the look of a man whose heart breaks even as he gazes, but to which he will not yield, he turned aside without so much as touching it, and she could more easily have died than called him back.

'Did I not see you conversing with some one, my dear?' said Lady Ann, appearing at her elbow as Madcap stood with fixed eyes that saw nothing.

She did not answer, only moved like an automaton; but on going home, went straight to her father, who was still pacing the library, his looks betraying the disorder that ruled his mind.

'Dad,' she said, 'I want to go home. May I go to-morrow?'

'Ay—go!' he said, pausing in his walk; 'and as soon as I have found this fellow—for the moment he stirs detectives will be on his track—I will follow you. Lady Ann can settle the affairs of the house; the others can follow later.'

'Thank you, father,' she said, but did not approach him, and sat alone with her heart for an hour, before any other eye saw her that day.

At luncheon she announced her intention, to Gordon's profound satisfaction, though less perhaps to that of Doune.

Matters between him and Nanciebel had not been brought to the happy conclusion that all lookers-on, save Madcap, had daily expected.

Doune was not the man to brook a refusal, and Nanciebel was not one to court an offer, and only gave him just enough encouragement to keep him from starving. Assured of his heart, she dallied with her happiness, and perhaps was wise in that she prolonged that most perfect period of love when each knows himself beloved of the other, yet neither has made the confession that, however divinely satisfying, is less exquisite than the yearning imagination has painted it. Perhaps the tantalizing sips of sweetness she had vouchsafed satisfied him more than she imagined; perhaps a girl's blue eyes will sometimes reveal her without her knowledge, or the inflection of a tone unconsciously betray her. But be this as it may, Doune wore no willow airs, and indeed looked so handsome and happy that Madcap often wondered what unseen influence it was that worked with such satisfactory results.

Neither had she yet discovered the object of Nanciebel's affection, though she was sure he existed, from the fact of that young woman's refusing two excellent matches on such frivolous grounds as an unsymmetrical body in the one instance, and a tendency to drink in the other.

She was thinking of Nanciebel then, as Lady Ann murmured gently about the responsibility of all Madcap's broken engagements, leave-takings, etc.; yet in her heart thought things might have been worse, pluming herself on the skill with which she had piloted so great a prize through so brilliant a season, only to find Gordon's right unchallenged at its end.

'I shall be able to get down by the day after to-morrow,' said Gordon cheerfully, 'so you won't be left very long by yourself.'

'Do not come,' said Madcap earnestly, and then he looked at her more closely, and saw that she was troubled. 'It will take a little while to get rid of your horses; and I want to be perfectly quiet, and left to myself for a day or two.'

'Well, I shall go down the moment I

have done my business,' said Gordon, looking crestfallen, in spite of his words; 'surely there is room enough for us both in Lovel?'

'When does Nanciebel come?' said Doune; and Madcap must have been deaf, surely, not to read his heart by the mere way he pronounced that name.

'I asked her from the first week in August.'

'Couldn't you persuade her to go down sooner?' said the young man quietly.

'I dare say. But not yet; not for a little while!' and with almost a wild gesture, Madcap rose from her place and went to the window, but in a moment she had returned.

'I think I am tired out,' she said, with the ghost of a smile; 'it is quite time that I went home. I am going to Nanciebel now, and I will ask her to come to us as soon as—as—I am better.'

'Poor little soul!' said Gordon, as the door closed on Madcap; 'a month more of this confounded gaiety would have killed her, I do believe. Well—she shan't come up to town next season, if *I* can help it!' and he went off whistling, and treading on air.

Madcap found Nanciebel in despair, and Mrs. Burgoyne's household in an active state of preparation for immediate departure.

Accident and a sanitary inspector combined, had just discovered that the house was fashionably built over a cesspool, and while one servant was down with typhoid, all the others, and their mistress as well, were frantic to be gone. Now Mrs. Burgoyne had for years endeavoured each year to tear herself from town delights, and take that journey to Marienbad which, for her figure if not her health's sake, was imperative; but now her opportunity had arrived, and on the following day she and Nanciebel were to set out. It would be hard to say which was the paler of the two usually blooming girls as they kissed each other; but between their degrees of suffering, comparison there was none.

Madcap's heart was a stone. Nancy's was merely torn with the thought of separation from Doune, without those words being said that she had so often checked, but now so desperately longed to hear. Had she not been looking forward, as he did, to her visit to the Red Hall? nay, had not the same thought trembled in her mind as his, that *there* he should ask his question, and she would give him his reply?

Madcap, shrouded in her own thoughts, faintly wondered at Nanciebel's distress; and glancing beyond her present misery, vaguely felt that she would miss the solace of the girl's companionship, for she had come to love her very dearly. Nor, when a servant entered to say Mr. Doune Eyre waited below on Miss Nanciebel, did the girl's quickly dried tears, her joyous trembling look, enlighten her—nay, so preoccupied was she, that she followed her down, and the two entered the room together.

Doune had already heard of the impending departure from Mrs. Burgoyne, who had discreetly left the room when she sent the message to Nanciebel, and was now figuratively washing her hands of the girl since her future seemed so brilliantly assured.

He came forward instantly, and took Nancy's little trembling hand; then, without a word to her, turned to Madcap, and said:

'She must not go to Marienbad—she can come to us at the Towers immediately, instead of later.'

Something in his voice pierced the insensibility that closed her in, as if a brick wall had been built up between her and the outer world, and looking from one to the other, at last she learned the truth. She received it without surprise or sign of any kind; then said:

'Yes—come; but not for three days.'

Doune had been holding Nancy's hand during this time, but he said no more to her than his eyes could speak, and Madcap perhaps wondered (with a curious sense of remoteness from all human interests) why this happy young pair had nothing to say to each other, and looked so grave.

Perhaps surprise even roused her a little, when, five minutes later, Mrs. Burgoyne having given consent, and all arrangements being made for Miss Nancy's housing during the three days before her departure for Lovel, she witnessed between the lovers a parting so unconcerned, so brief, that one might have sworn there was no serious feeling between them.

# BOOK IV.

## CHAPTER I.

*'Her heart and she.'*

MADCAP had walked and talked with her heart a night and a day, and it ached all the harder —it cried out to her all the louder as its complaint grew, and she had no power to still it; and the old familiar home only made her think of how happy her mother had been in it, with a man more than twice her own age.

Ay! but Mr. Eyre had loved her, and this man—her father's enemy—could expatriate himself rather than forget an old grudge. . . . 'Oh! this was not love, not love! It might be honour, but it was not love,' cried out the girl, as alone at night, in the room that had once been her nursery, she stood looking out at the moon-washed woods of Lovel below.

That very look had been summoned to his eyes by the revelation in her own, just as his mere glance had touched her heart with unbidden fire, and kindled it to a passion that terrified her; for, however sweetly cherished in her maiden thoughts he might have been this many a year, she had till then been as ignorant of *love's* true image as if she had never heard its name.

But the flame must have smouldered long, perhaps from that earliest day when she had unconsciously placed him in Frank's place, and in some curious way worshipped the two men in one.

Perhaps if she had never seen him more, he might in time have dwindled to a mere memory, about which clung her tenderest thoughts, her brightest dreams; but that chance meeting with him in the Park, that subsequent one on the Derby Day, had so filled her mind with his presence, that insensibly he had come to be the foremost image in it; and it only needed a last encounter by the rose-bush to make her betray herself.

What was he doing now? Pitying her? But no! no! 'He loved me, though he left me,' she cried, living over again that one moment of perfect happiness that was at least her own, and never to be dimly guessed at, and longed after, as by those poor hungry souls to whom such a moment has never come.

Had there not been agony in his face as

he took that last look at her, and turned away; had not the strength of his renunciation been but one degree more powerful than his longing to obey her bidding, and 'stay'?

Middle-aged, friendless, alone, how far had he gone, she wondered, on that long, long, journey, from which there could never be a home-coming? Was he thinking of her now? was he looking back, and in spirit keeping tryst with her at the gate where, as child and man, they had met and parted, and where the seed was sown that had burst, full-blown, into flower, when, as man and maiden, they met three years later?

Unconsciously the girl stretched out her arms in the direction of the cowslip-meadow, and a wild longing to visit the spot seized her.

No ghost of murder, no memory of Dody climbing up them barefooted, with his birthday rose, followed her, as she fled down the old stone steps, and across the courtyard, being presently swallowed up in the shadows below.

Soon she emerged upon the cowslip-meadow, whose stubble lay like a sheet of molten silver, through which, in her white gown, she stepped like a ghost, or some pale spirit that comes stealing to revisit the place on earth where it had found, and perchance lost, its life's treasure.

But within a few yards of the gate she paused, and putting one arm before her eyes, went by instinct the remaining steps; then dropping her head upon the topmost bar, suddenly realized, as she had not done before, to what utter ruin her life had come . . . for the young heart looks its shipwreck in the face so much more hopelessly than the older one does, since the old have known the joys that the young have never tasted, and the middle-aged stand half-way between happiness and its memory.

No thought of her father or of Doune came to Madcap then; the sweet, the bitter, the madness and ecstasy of love had swept body and soul in one passionate chord that made thought or consciousness impossible save of *him*; and that truest essence of the passion which makes a woman identify herself with the man she loves, whether in his humiliation or his triumph, his gladness or his sorrow, burned in Madcap's breast as she followed him in thought to the solitude to which he had condemned himself.

Probably no true woman ever contemplates, even in thought, the sufferings of the man she loves, as easily as she endures her own; and soon Madcap's arm was wet with the tears that her own agony had no power to bring forth, while her slender body shook with the violence of her sobs.

Suddenly she looked up, and saw on the other side of the gate, apart and alone, the ghost of the man to whose flesh and blood image she had bid farewell nigh on three days ago; and no shock of fear thrilled her as, all disordered with love and sorrow, they gazed upon each other, neither seeming to breathe, lest the spell that had summoned each to each should be broken!

Timidly she stretched out a pale hand as though to touch him, then drew it back, but not for fear, and looked again with such transfigured eyes of love as to man or spirit must have told their tale; and never, I wis, did disembodied spirit look such longing, passionate tenderness upon his sweetheart in the body, as did this lover, who stood but a yard away, yet would not, dared not, advance one step to meet her.

How clearly the mingled gold and the grey of his hair shone out in the moonlight; how stalwart and strong and brave his shape, with the head slightly downbent, and his face pale as her own in the moonbeams! But even as she gazed, he seemed to recede, and a black cloud obscuring the moon, his features faded from her sight; and ere she could cry out, or stir, he had receded into the gloom of the wood behind him, and with madly beating heart she was left to persuade herself that it was all a dream.

But the next moment she had pushed the gate wide, and without a thought of shame, or any other conscious thought but that she must find him, she fled on through the soft darkness that was all latticed and barred with silver; at first in silence, then, as the sense of loneliness deepened, whispering his name, 'Frank! Frank!' just as if she had known and called him by no other all her life!

So had she never thought of him till now, but in the spirit he would hear and understand her. . . . gradually her voice grew fainter, and she ceased to call him, coming back slowly to the cowslip-gate, through which she passed with a long sobbing sigh that reached the ears of one who thought an angel with the faithfulness of a woman had passed that way to-night.

## CHAPTER II.

'*What harm, my lord, provokes thine ire
To wreak itself on me?
Have I not saved thy life from foes,
And saved for sic a fee?*'

NO such excitement had been known in Lovel for many years as that which agitated it during the two days that preceded Madcap's arrival. Hester Clarke, long since supposed to be dead, had returned; and though absent nigh on a score of years, had been at once recognised, and received with a warmth that betokened the attitude of the village opinion towards her.

No matter if she came so secretly that none, save her old friend, knew of her presence till accident discovered her to be at Synge Lane; no matter if she never stirred abroad, and shrank even from the honest hands thrust forth to welcome her, crying out that she was not worthy to take them, for there was not a man or woman in the village who did not reckon her sins as white to the scarlet of those committed by the master of the Red Hall.

She volunteered no account of herself, and gave no reason for her visit; though some found it in the arrival, on the next day but one, of a gentleman who went straight to Synge Lane and remained at Hester's lodging some two hours, though where he went afterwards, nobody noticed, for just then Madcap drove through the village, and in the universal delight and astonishment, Hester and her possible lover were forgotten. But if her lover, why did she bring him *here*, to the scene of her greatest misery and degradation? And this man was a gentleman, with a curious resemblance to the Lovels, as more than one observed when he strode quickly past the gossips, looking neither to the right nor left, and more as if he were going to his own funeral (as one of the women afterwards said) than a-courting. 'Though what should two such middle-aged folk have to do with courting?' said the young girls, tossing their heads, and more alive to the disgrace than the pity of Hester's part in the great tragedy whose closing scenes had even yet to be played out.

But if lovers, then they chose a strange place later in the evening for exchanging their vows, since the village pedagogue, intent on star-gazing, came upon the pair as they stood side by side at Mrs. Eyre's grave. Now if the worthy man had one faculty in use beyond that of imparting learning, it was the faculty of never forgetting a face from its wrinkled infancy to a less wrinkled old age; and at sight of Hester's companion, he, without a second of hesitation, respectfully saluted him as Lord Lovel.

'Lord Lovel lies there,' said the man addressed, pointing to the grave on Madcap's left; and being but of a poor heart and easily abashed, the pedagogue slipped aside, and sat down on a tombstone out of sight, to reason out the problem of a dead man having his living effigy standing just over his head.

The moon had not fully risen, the tombstone was nearer to the pair than they supposed; and the pedagogue caught a word here and there that only added to the bewilderment of his mind.

What was it that had been done, and must still be done, 'for her sake'? What did a man mean who said he was leaving of his own free will, and for ever, the only thing he valued upon earth? And if Hester were his sweetheart, and he were leaving *her*, why didn't he give her a kiss by way of consolation? To be sure, he heard some words urging her to leave the village as soon as possible, in case of Mr. Eyre's accidental return, and to leave no trace by which she might be followed; but if this were not Lord Lovel's ghost in the flesh who should he be, to have so intimate a knowledge of Mr. Eyre's feelings towards her? Lastly he saw Hester stoop down and press her lips to the turf above the older Madcap's grave, and then the two went slowly away towards the village.

And so it happened that another besides Madcap saw a ghost in Lovel that night.

\*    \*    \*    \*    \*

Madcap had fallen asleep, still enwrapped in the magic shroud of her illusions; but with the morning light it fell from her, and looking back on her passionate exaltation of mood the night before, she recognised it as madness, and ran to her mirror to discover the signs of it in her face. But she found no madness there, only an odd sort of resemblance to her father that showed itself in moments of strong excitement; and she turned aside with a sob of relief to the open window, looking out to where far below spread that softly-swelling sea of green, beneath whose boughs she had pursued her mad love-chase overnight.

For she had *seen* him—whether in the flesh or the spirit, she had seen him. And had she indeed by pure longing found power to summon to her his outward presentment, though to her outstretched hand, her voice, he had remained insensible as the dead? And if his spirit, then he must have died, and none should blame her for summoning him to that midnight tryst; but if indeed she had seen him in the flesh, then he loved her not, but had fled from the sound of his own name as it followed him through the wood.

'*Frank! Frank!*' Her own voice seemed to thunder in louder and louder echoes through the silvery aisles; the very rustle of the leaves, the very pattern of their dance upon the sward seemed to whisper,

'He heard you calling—calling! And you will overtake him never—never!'

Shame seized Madcap, and for awhile cast out love. Had not her eyes sufficiently betrayed her, that she must shout her secret to the ears of a man whose only method of lovemaking had from the first been retreat?

While shame lasted, the scorpions of memory stung her, and she suddenly remembered that this man was avowedly her father's enemy. And what had the dear old father—her playmate, companion, friend—done, that Major Methuen should so hate, and at the same time avoid him?

From the first Mr. Eyre's attitude had been one of candour towards this double of Frank Lovel; he had sought sedulously as any beggar for an interview with him, and the evasions, the subterfuges that had prevented it, most assuredly did not lie at his door. The dishonour lay, then, with the man who persisted in a dishonourable silence; and gradually there grew in Madcap's breast a more intolerable pang far than when she had blushed for herself; *now* she blushed for the man she loved.

If only she might see him once more—take back by look and gesture the guerdon she had unasked bestowed upon him! But that was not likely now; by this time he had retreated far beyond the sound of a voice that plained and sobbed after him, like a forsaken bird that will not be consoled until it has found its mate.

Anger dried the tears in her eyes, and pride dressed her beautifully for breakfast, and that descent afterwards to the village for which every cottager confidently looked. But when she started, it was by way of the coppice and past the smithy, so that she entered the village almost unobserved, and more by accident than intention turned down Synge Lane.

The little cottage that boasted the only lodgings to let in Lovel, stood back from its garden, and the house-door being open, Madcap entered, then stopped short, as from a room within Major Methuen's voice struck on her ear.

The coldness towards him that had so rapidly grown within her, strengthened to ice as a woman's voice followed on his in accents of passionate pleading, of which the sound but not the sense reached her brain.

Noiselessly as she had come, so she departed. So this was the 'last farewell' that Major Methuen had to take before he left England for ever; and it was in the keeping of this appointment that he had accidentally strayed towards the cowslip-gate overnight. Oh, fool! to think that for his *friend's* sake he was leaving her! Oh, fool! to have mistaken him for her lover!

The women that morning found Madcap beautiful, praised her colour and her dress, but of village gossip told her not one word.

'Who is lodging in Synge Lane?' she said at last, and saw how looks were exchanged, heads nodded, while an indescribable air of confusion came upon the group addressed.

'It's a young woman, miss,' said Sal of the mill, stepping into the breach. 'She's only here for a bit—just to meet her young man,' she added in a flash of inspiration; 'and I reckon the pair of 'em 'll be gone before long.'

'Who is the young man?' said Madcap,

reading accurately enough the stolid faces around her, and convinced that they were keeping something from her; 'and who is the young woman?'

'Well, she ain't young, miss, so to speak, for she's nigh on forty; and she's called Hester. And the young man, he's not young either; but they're just as handsome a pair as ever stood together.'

'They are old friends?' said Madcap.

'Yes, miss,' said the woman slowly and cautiously. 'Many and many years ago, before you was born, folks called 'em lovers; and now it seems like as if they had made up their minds to be happy.'

'Have their lives, then, been so wretched?' exclaimed Madcap, pale and cold, but with no other outward sign of the heart that was breaking in her breast.

'They've had trouble,' said Sal cautiously;

but before she could think of further details with which to embroider her daring invention, Madcap had turned away as if weary of the subject.

'What ever made you tell her that lie?' said one of the women in a whisper to Sal; 'if she sees him, she'll see quick enough he's a gentleman, and not for the likes of Hester. But the Lord save her if the master comes down unexpected, and finds her in the place!'

'She'll be off like a swallow now Miss Madcap's come,' said another. 'But she'll get a look at her first, and 'twill scare her —just as if 'twas Mrs. Eyre rose from the dead.'

'Look!' exclaimed Sal in an awe-struck whisper, and pointing towards the entrance to Synge Lane, whence two figures were emerging; 'they're coming, and she doesn't see them, for she's talking to Goody Holt. But what's the matter with him? He's looking at Miss Madcap as if he knew her, and now she's looking too. There! off goes his hat, and she's speaking, and Hester's like to faint. And now they've took the road to the station, and Miss Madcap's going home by the copse.

'Lord!' said Goody Holt a few moments later to her gossips, 'how proud Miss Madcap have growed in Lunnun! She just said "Good-morning, sir!" as if he was dirt, and without a glint of her eye on his face; and she looked at Hester, poor soul, as if she'd been p'ison!'

## CHAPTER III.

*''Tis not the frost that freezes fell,*
*Nor blawing snaw's inclemencie;*
*'Tis nae sic cauld that makes me cry,*
*But my love's heart grown cauld to me.*

'MADCAP!'

'Gordon!'

'Yes, here I am,' said the young man guiltily; 'but I thought you might be dismal here by yourself—and, by Jove, you look so!' he added, with sudden concern; 'you are as white as your frock!' and he touched one of her flounces of muslin embroidery.

'And may I not be as pale as I please,

here, where I came on purpose to be *quiet?*' said Madcap, with an angry stamp of her little foot.

'You seem to have had visitors, all the same,' said Gordon drily, 'for I don't suppose Methuen came to call on anyone in the village. Perhaps it's part of his game at General Post to come down here when he knows your father is looking for him in town.'

'Where did you see him?' said Madcap, continuing the task in which Gordon had surprised her, and which happened to be that of dusting and arranging her father's books.

'He got into the train that I got out of,' said Gordon, 'and stared at me as if he saw a ghost.'

'There is nothing on earth that you less resemble,' said Madcap; 'and you are wrong in supposing he came to look for father or me,' she added below her breath, 'for he came on a visit to a person in the village. And how is Nancichel?' she added, with an abrupt change of tone.

'I don't know, and I don't care,' said the young fellow, and snatched her duster and threw it down; then caught her hands and held them.

'Madcap,' he said, 'for once and all, you shall give me my answer to-day.'

She looked up, and the ardent love, the power, the protection of Gordon's look and attitude could not but strike her, in contrast with the cold neglect, the outrage, that the man she loved had put upon her.

'Oh, Gordon!' she said, and somehow realized that here was her mother's story with Frank Lovel over again; and something in her voice—more of pity for herself than him—struck the young fellow oddly, and he put her back the better to search her face.

'Who is it?' he said, pain hardening his voice, and for once making it masterful.

The colour flew into her face, the light to her eyes in that moment; however it might disgrace her, flesh and blood bore witness to the truth of how

> '*In her heart a grace hath reigned,
> That nothing else could bring* . . .'

and Gordon read the signs surely and truly. He dropped her hands, and went to the window, coming back just as she stooped to pick up her duster.

'He loves you?' he said, still in that stern voice so unfamiliar to Madcap's ears.

'No.'

'Then God help you, Madcap!' he said, and went out; and mechanically she echoed his words, and shivered with a sense of cold as she stood alone.

Was she to be left by everyone — by Doune, by Gordon, by *him*—(ah! this last was the bitterest stab of all, with a bow and a 'Good-morning, sir!' to represent their leavetaking)—by all save the dear old dad, whom she had betrayed when she loved his enemy?

She knelt down by his chair, but even as she put her lips to the leather, knew that however faithfully he had loved her, he was not first with her now. She could think of him tenderly; she was vaguely conscious of clinging to him as her one refuge in the future, but for the moment she felt only a raging desire to be alone, beyond human sight or sound of human voices, confronting the fact that Major Methuen not only loved and rode away, but rode away with another woman. Her cool green hollow beckoned her, even across blinding fields of heat; and it was safe, it was secret. The only soul who knew of its existence was by now far away, and Gordon might search the woods for a month before ever he found it and her.

She caught up her white sunshade, and went by the way that she had passed overnight, shame stinging her at every step freshly, as she thought of how swiftly she had sped to the one-sided tryst in which she had taken passionate farewell of a ghost that in point of fact was a very substantial body running away.

She laughed aloud, climbed to her seat, and looked down the long and beautiful aisles that she had so long reckoned her own, and which Major Methuen had also seemed to think at his disposal. Then, the moment having at last come when she was alone with her misery and her shame, turning her cheek to the moss of the tree, Madcap wept.

She cried out no more than her father would have done under equal punishment, but her body trembled as if shaken by a violent hand; and was it a ghost that in the afternoon sunshine drew near, and stood looking down on her with such misery in his eyes as her hidden ones could not have matched?

So had he seen her mother once, and a word from him had ended that one short, bitter space of a sunny life, and she had been happy, happy afterwards to the very end; and now a word from him would save her child, and he neither willed nor dared to speak it.

For himself he hardly thought; just as

he had foregone his happiness and good
name in the past, now he forewent his
happiness in the future: but for every
pang that he had suffered for Madcap the
elder, he suffered a thousand now, as he
watched the convulsed form from which
there came neither sound nor sob, though
the sod alone knew what bitter tears fell
from the eyes pressed close above them.

And she wept for *him*; though his heart
half broke to see her suffer, yet exultation
swelled it—just as that divine revelation of
her love, when they had met by the rose-
bush, had at once electrified and stunned
him; for hopelessly, passionately as he
loved her, he had never looked for or expected any return in kind, and beneath that
heavenly shock, body and soul had cried
out fiercely against duty when she had bid
him 'stay.' And he had wrestled with

the temptation, and cast it out; he had put this most exquisite moment of his life almost untasted by, and thanklessly as a beggar into whose hand has been ignorantly dropped a priceless gem, he had turned away, nor thanked her for that precious gift; nay, had he not even seemed to scorn her, when in that strange ghostly meeting in the moonlight he had fled from her out-stretched hand, and the sound of her sweet voice calling him through the wood!

The echo of those notes of love lingered in his ears yet . . . yet he had taken harsher ones with him when by sheer self-mastery he had forced himself from Lovel that day, only to find that his *will* compelled him to return; so that at the risk of his neck he had leaped from the train soon after it had cleared the station, and come straight hither, bent on one last secret look at her, one last unuttered farewell.

For fresh in his memory was her cold 'Good-morning, sir!' spoken with the fine air, too proud to be contempt, that certain women can assume at will, and that had set him at such a distance as to make him doubt if his eyes and ears had not played him false overnight; and he had half expected to find her indifferent to his departure, or at most but a little ashamed that she had forgotten her legitimate lover to exchange a look of love with a man old enough to be her father, and for whom she had always borne the affection of a friend.

But here, in this woodland recess, to which her childish hand had once guided him, she was herself, and unconsciously the true and tender heart was bared to his gaze. Perhaps some sense of the wrong he did her by his presence smote him, perhaps a sense that his strength was failing him made him resolute to leave her before he should be discovered; for with one last long look at the half-hidden face, one gesture as of despair towards her, he turned slowly away.

Something beneath his foot crackled, and she sprang up.

For a moment the gap between her thoughts of him in the spirit and his presence here in the flesh was not to be bridged . . . her tears froze, her sobs ceased, she stood still as a statue, each muscle tense and rigid as steel.

'Madcap!' he said.

His voice broke the spell; once more she breathed, and a faint colour overspread her features; but into her eyes came a look that fell on him chill as ice, as, scorning to hide the tears that blotted her face, she said:

'Have you Lord Lovel's permission to be here?'

Her voice was gentle, for Madcap was of the sort that can rail at herself, but not at her lover, or what she loves; and though anger alone at his intrusion then filled her mind, her eyes and lips told each a different tale.

'Yes; I have his permission.'

'Then I will leave you to enjoy it,' she said, and moved to depart.

What! had he not slighted her enough overnight? was not her very glance of love by the rose-bush won from her under false pretences, since he knew himself pledged to another woman, and that woman the same he had flaunted before her eyes to-day? I say, was not all this enough, without returning secretly to spy on her in this her most miserable hour?

'No, you will stay,' he said resolutely. 'And so you love me—I know it now.'

'That, sir,' she said with spirit, 'is a lesson very easily unlearned.'

'Is it?' he said. 'I have learned but one; for my love for you is but a continuation of the old.'

'Then Hester must be satisfied with a new,' said Madcap, with a half-mocking courtesy.

'Hester!' he exclaimed. 'What has she to do with me?'

'Nothing, except that she is your—sweetheart.'

'My sweetheart!' echoed Frank, an angry flush rising to his forehead. 'Who has told you such an insane story?'

But he got no answer. Madcap had

turned her head aside, that he might not see the joy that painted her face—joy, even though she knew that not all the weight of his love, nor hers, could bridge the gulf that divided them.

'And you believed it?' he said, perhaps never having felt the degradation of his position so keenly as then; 'and is that why you said "Good-morning, sir!" as if I were your footman?'

'Does one call one's footman "sir"?' said Madcap, half turning, and showing such happy dimples and eyes (still wet) of such pure content, as read him her heart more sweetly even than her tears had done.

'And you can be happy, Madcap!' he said, almost with a groan; 'and after to-day we shall never look upon each other's faces again.'

'Do we not love one another?' she said, at once proudly and gently; 'and is not that enough?'

'No, it is not enough for me,' he said, and drew his breath hard, looking at her with a hunger that would not be content with little, but must fill its soul, or famish; while in her eyes was the restful joy of a woman who is satisfied so long as she holds the one morsel she has coveted safe in her hand.

Perhaps no man ever really appreciates the unselfishness, the reticence, of a true woman's love; and Frank's voice was bitter as he repeated:

'It is not enough for me, and I cannot, *will* not let you go. If you had not loved me, I could have borne my lot, wretched though it might be; but duty is a poor thing when it demands the sacrifice of a life dearer than your own.'

'Then if dearer, it should be stronger in duty than yourself,' said Madcap firmly. 'Do you think I would have let you see my heart so plainly, given you my love *unasked*, if I did not know that we are eternally separated from each other? You should have sued to me long, had there been a chance—a chance——'

Her voice faltered, though a smile was on her lip, and pure and perfect as that first look of love which had revealed her to him by the rose-bush was the look in her eyes now, and a madness seized him, in which he said:

'There is a way—and only one.'

His gaze searched hers, as if to see what reserves of strength and courage lay behind her beauty and her love; as his face hardened beneath the urgency of his regard, so unconsciously did hers, till the girl's face was almost as resolute as the man's.

'You are strong,' he said, 'but your love must be stronger. Will you give up your father, brother, home, without a hope of ever seeing either again, to trust yourself *absolutely* to me?'

A cold breath seemed to pass through her as he spoke, for she was of the sort that could brook unfaith in her lover rather than his dishonour.

'Do you know what you are asking me to do?' she said, white as snow.

'To trust me all in all, or not at all.'

'Then,' she said, so low that he barely heard her, 'it must be not at all.'

But even as she spoke, the moment of madness passed, and he cursed himself for having vitiated in one moment of selfishness the abnegation of half a lifetime.

Cold and haggard, the fires in his eyes suddenly burnt out, he fearlessly lifted his head to her; and as their glance met, she asked herself if Nature had indeed lied when she stamped his features with such nobility, sincerity, and truth. No! Dishonour had laid no finger there, and if she might not trust him all in all, she would trust him yet.

She had risen from the seat that he and she had once filled like king and queen, and now he stood like a beggar below, though the boon that his soul desired was in sooth no poor one.

Perhaps she guessed it, as, his eyes compelling her, slowly she rose, and stooped to him . . . stooped lower yet, till her knees sank in the turf, and he could reach his arm to draw her down . . . together their lips mingled in the word 'good-bye' . . . and Madcap had kissed him.

## CHAPTER IV.

*'I mayna turn, I canna turn,
I daurna turn and fight with thee.'*

THE woodland life around beat not a pulse the slower or the quicker because a maiden had given her first kiss as easily as a chance common thing might, whose fancy had flamed up at the mere beckoning of a man's finger.

Yet no shame painted itself on the girl's pale cheek, but only fear, as the lips that had sought hers so eagerly grew cold as death, and the arm about her neck slipped, as without word or sigh he dropped insensible in the hollow below, and lay like a dead man, with one arm hanging curiously stiff and straight by his side.

In an instant Madcap was kneeling beside him and lifting it, but a touch told her that it was broken, and with a sob she laid it down.

Her voice roused him; he tried to rise, leaning his weight on the broken limb, but she cried out in horror, and lent him all her strength, so that she seemed to be clasping him in her arms, as for a second they stood together.

'*Frank!*' exclaimed a terrible voice behind them, and Madcap shrank back, as at last Mr. Eyre and the man she loved stood face to face, every line distinct in the broad June sunshine.

'*Methuen!*' said the other doggedly.

'You lie!' cried Mr. Eyre, with a gesture

as though he could have struck him across the mouth; 'it has been a lie, a deception, from the beginning, and I find you *here*, a coward to the last, and making for me traitors among even my own household!'

In his passion, he loathed his daughter too much to look at her, and so she was spared a glance that must have left its mark, for he thought her a partner in the whole fraud, and that by merest accident he had here surprised a long premeditated assignation.

But Madcap was one of those who can stand aside and wait, 'containing their souls,' and did not blench then, or after, through the closing scenes of the tragedy in which she had unconsciously played a part all her life.

'*Methuen*, at your service,' said the man

who stood at the foot of the beech-tree, his face set like a flint, his eyes hard as steel.

'By God!' cried Mr. Eyre, 'either you or I shall not leave this wood alive to-day, unless I drag from your lips the truth.'

'If you have weapons with you,' said the other, 'you may murder me; but you shall not force me to speak.'

'Murder you!' said Mr. Eyre, and looking at the man before him with bitterest hatred and loathing; 'have you not murdered *me*, body and soul? Have you not poisoned my life with a lie—written down a false accusation, and run away, fearing to face it out or hear my reply? To lie, to deceive, to suborn my very daughter —my only daughter; to take another man's name and wear it, deceiving the doting old mother of a dead man—to act from first to last a hideous lie—would *murder* be punishment enough for all this, coward, liar, *traitor?*"

With the last word he deliberately struck the man before him a heavy blow on the mouth, and as the blood sprang, Madcap trembled with pure feminine sickening at the sight of men in conflict, and ran forward, crying out, '*Father!*'

'You here?' he said, and turned on her a look beneath which she might well have cowered; 'get you home, and pray God to make you more like your mother.'

'She is dead!' said the girl, pale as snow, 'and my place is by you. It is all a mistake, and it is Major Methuen who stands there.'

She did not—*could* not lift her eyes to the man who had taken the blow so tamely; but Mr. Eyre thrust her away violently, and said, 'Home with you—home!' and with a sob as though he had beaten her, she turned and fled without one backward look; till, her foot catching in the root of a tree, she fell against its bole, and lay stunned, though whether for a moment or an hour she did not know.

When she came to herself, and looked around, she was far out of earshot, but within sight of the two men who now stood in the green hollow that had so long been her peaceful retreat; but their gestures, however controlled, expounded the *heart* tragedy in process of being enacted. . . Here was one of those awful scenes over which the pen falters, the brush fails, for only human voice and eye could adequately describe and see it; but out of its prolonged agony Mr. Eyre came forth victorious, and, having *torn* the truth bit by bit from his enemy, passed with features

> *Dim and dank and grey,*
> *Like a storm-extinguished day,*
> *Travelled o'er by dying gleams. . . .*

moving blindly, and with uncertain steps, towards home.

But he had not gone a score yards when his daughter's arms caught him, and he looked at her as one might at the long-forgotten dead . . . in the awful wrong he had done her mother, the girl's wrong-doing was extinguished; and he did not even remember his anger against her as they went a few steps along the way that with only anxious, not hopeless, hearts they had traversed such a short time ago.

'Child,' he said, stopping abruptly, 'take your hand from mine; it is red with blood —the blood of your mother.'

'Father!' she said, struck to the soul, and for a second recoiling from him beneath this upheaval of her whole life. . . .

'Ay—*your father*,' he said, looking down at his hand; 'for it seems a hand can work without *will*, knowledge, conscience. But Frank will tell you the whole story if you go to him.'

'*Frank?*' she repeated; then forgot the man whose name she uttered, as, crying out 'Father, *father!*' she only held closer that beloved figure . . . nothing that he might have done could touch the core of her allegiance, and without one backward look she led him away, and, with every step a pang, got him home to his library, where immediately he fell into a profound slumber.

He had walked by her side like an automaton, and laid himself down as one; and in the sleep or stupor into which he had fallen, his features retained the fearful expression that had been stamped on them during the interview in the wood.

Pale and cold for awhile, Madcap stood and watched him; but there was work to be done, and, calling Nan, she installed her in the remotest corner of the library, with orders not to move till she returned; then ran out with at once the quickest and heaviest feet that had ever carried her through the cowslip-gate, to the hollow in which she prayed as she went to find the man whom, of all upon earth, she most desired to see.

Long before she got within sight of it, she *felt* that he was there, and was by his side before he had lifted himself from the attitude of despair into which he had fallen when Mr. Eyre left him.

She could not see his face, which was to the tree; but his open hand held behind his back fixed her attention, and, leaning forward, she saw that on the inside of the thumb was a diamond-shaped scar.

The discovery gave her no shock. She was wholly possessed now with her father's state, and with no blush or thought of self, touched that hand and said:

'Lord Lovel!'

He turned and looked at her. Alas, alas! how quickly had love's bitter drowned in them both love's sweet! For he was paler than she, and so completely broken by the intense struggle of the past hour, that scarcely could his manhood command strength to look at her, and stand still to await her questions.

But the red mark on his mouth must have reminded her, if no inward thought had done, of her errand, and she said:

'You have tried to persuade my father that he killed my mother; and he is ill, nervous—angry with you for the deception you have practised towards him. But do you not know that my mother died in childbirth?'

'She did,' said the man before her; 'and Mr. Eyre is ill and unnerved, as you say. Do not listen to him—to-morrow he will think and speak differently.'

'No,' cried Madcap; 'I will have the *truth*—if you can speak it,' she added below her breath.

Had ever a man two such deadly pieces of work, with scarce a breath between, as had this one as he looked on the girl, and felt the second ordeal more terrible than the first?

As he had taken the blow, so he took the gibe—silently. Nigh on twenty years ago he had humbly imitated a Divine example, and taken up his burden without a groan; and now he waited, bringing his last remnants of courage and endurance to meet her next words.

'How *could* he be guilty?' she cried passionately. 'You make a wild accusation; but I know that you got a little touched in India, and so you have imagined things. . .'

He stood mute as a stone; for if he had often lied before for her mother's sake, here he *could* not, nor felt the same imperative need, since in this second Madcap was the strength to dare and do which had been denied to the older one.

'So you are all that my father called you,' she said at last, as he maintained that stubborn silence, and she saw how the short hair on his temples was dark and wet with the dews of agony; 'and all my life long I have been worshipping a hero only to find him something worse than a murderer—something that stabs in the dark and hides in the daylight—in one word, an *assassin!*'

The ugly word sped like a blow as she advanced a step, and looking at him with eyes grown hard and cold in an hour, virtually denied her love, and sided with her father against him.

He made a step forward as if to leave her, but she stood before him with flaming eyes, fired by a resolution that would have made her go through a dozen scenes more terrible than this, to save her father.

'His life is at stake,' she said; 'I saw death in his face when I left him. Tell me on what grounds you base your awful accusation, that I may prove to him you are *mad* when I go back.'

Here was a way out of the situation—to be *mad*, to feign forgetfulness of all that he had said and done; but, curiously enough, the man who in early youth could sacrifice his honour and see himself contemptible in the eyes of his first love, could not in middle age brook the same degradation in the eyes of his second and last sweetheart.

'I am not mad,' he said slowly; 'but if it will do your father any good to think me so——'

'Oh!' she cried, 'do you think that I have not strength to hear what is *killing* him?'

'It would kill you,' he said, 'and you are innocent; it is unnatural that you should suffer so; *his* is the sin, let *his* be the punishment.'

'The young die more easily than the old,' she said; 'tell me the whole story, for I must go back to *him* directly. . .'

To tell her the whole story . . . that story of a sin which even angels might not utter without tears of horror and pity . . . it was beyond his strength; and putting her aside almost as abruptly as her father had done, he was gone from her sight before she had time to stretch a hand or lift a voice to stay him.

## CHAPTER V.

*'Heaven cannot abide it,
Earth refuses to hide it . . .'*

MADCAP found the library sofa unoccupied, and no living soul in sight but Nan, who sewed her seam through mental shipwreck, as she would have sewn it through one at sea, so long as the light, or glare of torch-beams lasted.

Madcap shook the woman, in the agony of her fear; but Nan knew nothing of 'Master' except that he had suddenly woke up, and gone out on the instant, 'like one as walks in his sleep,' she added stolidly, not knowing how in her stupidity she had given a clue to the young mistress, who rushed away as on the wings of the wind.

All down the village she sped, with her eager question of 'Have you seen my father?' and having easily tracked him to Synge Lane, rejoiced to see his back through the uncurtained window, in conversation, as she supposed, with his tenant.

She drew in her breath with a half sob as she entered the open door, scarce knowing what she had dreaded in her delight at having found him, but paused on the very threshold of the room, as certain words reached her ears, spoken in an unfamiliar voice.

'I came down here,' it said, 'to look at the Pool, and think of my sin; for I knew you were safe in town, and I never expected to see Lord Lovel.'

'So, in tracking *him* hither, I have found you both,' said Mr. Eyre; 'and you and I are face to face at last—and if Frank Lovel *thought* he spoke the truth to me this afternoon, you shall substantiate it.'

'What could he tell you more than you know already?' said the woman's voice; 'have not both he and I bound ourselves as exiles to save you? Neither of us came back till we thought you absent or dead; and for your child's sake—made in *her* image—we both willingly effaced ourselves again.'

'Good God!' cried Mr. Eyre; 'have you, too, taken leave of your senses—do *you* suppose that I murdered my wife?'

'I *saw* you kill her,' said the woman's voice beyond. 'O Heavens! if only I might have saved her . . . but I was barely in time to see it, and the window was between——'

'*Liar!*' he cried; 'confess that you yourself committed the crime, and bear false witness against me but to save yourself. But this time there shall be no miscarriage of justice, and you shall hang for her murder yet.'

'I would hang willingly,' said the voice, 'for the sin is mine, and she never wronged me; my wretched weakness was at the root of all, and perhaps you did well to slay her —she is happier as she is.'

'What! you still persist in that horrible lie?' he cried, in a voice of fury, 'the poisonous lie that drove Lord Lovel forth, that, on his return, you have instilled into his ear drop by drop, till his very soul is drugged with its untruth? Before my God

I will swear that this right hand is *innocent* of her blood as——'

'Stay!' cried the voice; 'do not perjure yourself so; these eyes *saw* that hand commit the crime, and to avoid giving evidence against you I ran away, but was drawn back by my love for your child, and when you committed me for trial I resolved that, if convicted, I would die *silent*.'

'Silent?' cried Mr. Eyre; 'then how came Lord Lovel by his knowledge?'

'In your brain fever you revealed everything,' said the woman; 'until then he believed me guilty—and I did not undeceive him.'

Mr. Eyre laughed aloud—and to one of the hearers it sounded like that of a mocking devil, and to the other that of a madman, as she crouched with her brow to the lintel of the half-opened door.

'Does a man in brain-fever speak the truth?' he said contemptuously; 'and as to your *eyes*—who would trust them, with a knowledge of your antecedents? The brain that could plan a murder could easily enough plan a lie.'

There was no answer, no sound of any kind but that of Mr. Eyre's steps as he paced to and fro about the narrow room; but when those steps stopped, Madcap's heart seemed stopped also, as she waited for his next words.

'You have impressed your lie vividly enough upon Lord Lovel; tell it to *me*, and with some circumstantial detail, that I may the more readily appreciate it——'

'Have you *forgotten* it?' cried the woman, with a passion of wonder in her voice; 'how you came up the winding stair from the library, and, pausing at sight of the seated figure, snatched a knife from the open dressing-case and stabbed her savagely to the heart as she sat asleep by the window, before I could even cry out? You left her there for dead, and thrust the knife away in a cabinet, and went downstairs as one who walks in his sleep, and I was frozen, and could not call out or stir; but presently my senses came back, and I cried "*Murder!*" hoping that she was not dead.'

'And the scrap of your clothing found attached to her chair—what of that?' said Mr. Eyre.

'I had forced my way through the narrow window; I was feeling her heart, her pulse, when the light of your candle showed zigzag on the private stair, and at the same moment came the sound of hurrying feet; some impulse made me snatch the knife from the cabinet in which I had seen you place it, and I escaped barely in time, only to be intercepted by Digges at its foot. I struggled with him and got away, stumbling on for miles, till I thought myself safe from pursuit. But the child drew me back; suddenly it was borne in upon me that he was very ill, and in the dead of night I returned to find him dying in Lord Lovel's arms. But he died *in mine*—thank God for that—my little love, my angel! and as he lay dead upon my knees, you entered with the officers of the law, and ordered them to take me to prison, charged with the murder I had seen you commit.'

Mr. Eyre suddenly burst out into a fit of violent, shocking laughter, that revealed his state of incipient madness more clearly than a thousand other extravagances could have done.

'So that is the story into which you have persuaded Frank Lovel!' he said; 'this is the tissue of lies that you have taken seventeen years to build up! But a judge and jury will find out these, for to-morrow morning I will give myself up to justice, on your evidence, as the murderer of my wife.'

'No, no!' cried Hester passionately. 'You have forced—*wrung* the truth from me; but for *her* sake—for the sake of the vow I made to her the day before she died —I would hang for your crime rather than publicly accuse you of it!'

'No,' said Mr. Eyre; 'you would only slay my soul, as my *friend* has done. But each syllable that you and he have spoken to-day shall be sifted in a court of law; for by the God against whom I have sinned, I *swear* that this hand is innocent of my wife's blood!'

In the awful silence that followed, Madcap's heart seemed to cease to beat, and the very life-blood to ebb from her veins. Then came the sound of a woman's sob—hard, anguished, as the last hopeless cry of a profound despair.

'Ay, weep if you can,' said Mr. Eyre, in a terrible voice: 'you, who destroyed the happiness, took the life of the sweetest soul God ever made; for if your *hand* hesitated to slay her, your deeds stood fast to break her heart, and but for you she would be living still.'

'I know it,' said Hester, in a voice scarcely less unnatural than his. 'It was *my* sin, *my* weakness, that brought about the whole tragedy from first to last; and that's why I let you accuse me falsely; that's why I would have died without speaking, if they had brought me in guilty at the trial—for *her* sake and Dody's; and because she loved you . . . and it was the only way I could make it up to her . . . though she's happy now, for she has got *him*——'

The woman's voice broke and became human; tears came, and relieved her. But Mr. Eyre, dry-eyed, incredulous, yet shaken to the very centre of his being, laughed again as he looked at her.

'You and my Lord Lovel have managed it very well between you,' he said; 'you must have had many interviews, to dovetail your stories so circumstantially; but I find more than one flaw in your ingenious narrative—though the best legal talent in England will discover them without *my* help before I am a week older.'

'Yes,' said Hester; 'Lord Lovel and I have managed *well*, as you say. What he learned, he learned from your lips alone in your delirium; then we combined, and decided on your account to live as exiles.'

'Say on your *own!*' cried Mr. Eyre furiously, as one whose endurance fails him; 'a pair of traitors, who deserve to die a hundred deaths to avenge her *one!* But this time you shall not escape me;' and he strode to the door, and was about to call to the woman of the house, when he stumbled over Madcap's body, as she kneeled with her brow to the lintel, pale, and with a look of death imprinted on her features.

He stooped to lift her, and carried her in . . . if he could have uttered sob or cry, as Hester had done but now. his agony might have been less; but grim and silent he sat down with his burden, and only looked at her . . . here was his punish ment; here, in the suffering of this innocent soul, he found the chastisement that he had impiously denied his Maker; and in that moment (though unconsciously to himself) the core of his heart became *human*, and as a child who bows to the rod, so bowed he then to the hand of God.

Hester had drawn near . . . nor years, nor loss, nor anguish, could stifle in her that throb of motherhood which had governed the greater part of her life; and in this pale, still shape she seemed to see once more the Madcap whose life she had cut short by her sin . . . seemed to see chances of redemption even thus late in the day, though she might *now* do no more than kneel to kiss the pale hand that hung down, and which Mr. Eyre instantly snatched away, as if the woman's touch were pollution.

Madcap opened her eyes on the instant, blaming herself for lack of courage; and meeting Hester's gaze, and reading its perfect truth, sealed one of those silent compacts that between true and generous souls are seldom broken; then took her father's hand, and said:

'Dad, take me home.'

The familiar epithet, used through all the seventeen years of her beautiful childhood's love and trust in him, moved Mr. Eyre naturally and profoundly . . . for a moment his iron features relaxed, but the next he put her aside, and turned to Hester.

'You will consider yourself under arrest,' he said; 'and until I can secure assistance I will myself remain to watch you. And now, child, if you are able, get home with you; and since this confounded woman of

the house seems to be absent, send down
some people from the Hall.'

Disobedience had never been bred in
Madcap's nature, but for a moment she
paused, and thought deeply; then, with a
gesture to Hester that Mr. Eyre did not see,
went out, only to meet, on the threshold of
the open door, Lord Lovel.

'I was going to look for you,' she said,
without a thought of self, and as a soul
might speak which has lost its body; 'there
is some frightful mistake here . . . for she
speaks the truth, and so does my father;
and between them——'

'So here are more secrets,' said Mr. Eyre's
voice behind them; and his glance fell cold
as ice on his daughter. 'There seems to be a
conspiracy among you; but a man is mostly
betrayed by his nearest and dearest. And
here is my tenant,' he added, as a woman

came up the narrow garden, exhausted by the unusual business of a day spent in Marmiton, no more expecting thieves than debtors at the humble house that was left on the latch, morning, noon, and night.

Madcap stood between the two men whom she loved best upon earth, her heart torn between them, now espousing this side, now that, but firm in faithfulness to her father, whom she was resolved to save, though *how* was a question of the future.

'Your servant, miss,' said the woman, curtseying low to Madcap and looking coldly at Mr. Eyre. 'I left my house empty, but I find it full,' and she turned a curious look on Lord Lovel as she spoke.

'Look you,' said Mr. Eyre, 'the woman in that room yonder is a *prisoner*, and you will see to it that she does not escape.'

'And the charge against her, sir?' said the mistress of the house.

'False accusation and bearing of false witness,' said Mr. Eyre grimly; 'but you are in her pay, and not to be trusted. And so you must go home, Madcap,' he added, as he drew out his pocket-book, 'and send a servant off on horseback at once with these instructions;' and he wrote them down with a firm hand, and gave her the torn-out leaf without a tremor.

She took it as calmly as he gave it, not knowing whence came the reserves of strength that enabled her to meet this fearful hour; but, looking at him as she turned away, saw a sudden, terrible change in his face, and was barely in time to catch him as he fell, swaying slowly as some mighty monarch of the woods that quivers as with a mortal agony ere it crashes heavily to the earth.

But Madcap was young and strong to love and save, and she neither sobbed nor cried out, as, with Frank's help, they two bore that beloved body up, the one his head and the other his feet, and carried him in, and laid him down where he seemed to lie in a deep slumber, that was neither a natural one, nor yet a swoon or stupor. But to Madcap's mind a sentence of Hester Clarke's was working to the exclusion of every other thought or outward impression: '*He went downstairs as one who walks in his sleep.*' . . . Suddenly she drew her hand from her eyes, to see Frank standing near, and looking at her earnestly.

'Leave me now,' she said. 'There is something that I must think out. I must save him. But do not go away from the house, for you must help me to get him home presently.'

He went without a word—what could any human being do for her in such an hour as this? She drew down the thick green blind to shut out the sunshine, and seated herself in the twilight thus made near the window, unconsciously occupying the same chair, and in the same attitude, as Hester Clarke had filled on a certain fatal night, over seventeen years ago.

'*As one who walks in his sleep*' . . . and from childhood Doune, who in mind and body was Mr. Eyre's younger *replica*, had walked in his, and had once startled his sister by coming to her room at midnight, light in hand, and, sitting down at her table, read from a favourite book till dawn, when, replacing the volume, he went away, though next morning he recollected nothing of the occurrence, and declared she had been dreaming.

She bowed her head upon her hands, and prayed for a sign; and even as she prayed, it came, for Mr. Eyre, waking suddenly, and seeing that seated white figure in the gloom beyond, advanced towards it with fury, and lifted his hand violently, as if in act to strike it.

But as she looked up, and he saw the features of wife and daughter in one, he stepped back, for he had found the lost link in his memory that had escaped him seventeen years . . . he had desired to kill Hester, and he had killed . . . no, no! it was impossible; yet this last accident had determined the course of his already unsettled reason, and, before Madcap could reach him, he had opened the door, and was gone.

There was a short cut from Synge Lane

to the Hall, and this he took, while Madcap followed at a distance, dreading to startle him, yet nourishing in her heart a clue to what might be his redemption . . . and behind her again came Frank, while in the cottage two women clung together as straws caught in the eddy of a whirlpool.

The sun was setting in a fashion that betokened storm. Massed clouds of magenta and purple were piled high above a sea of palest green that melted imperceptibly into rose, which burned again into vivid gold, then flamed into red, while to right and left stretched vast plains of mingled hues that contrasted strongly with an ebony cloud, through which there showed from time to time little lovely islets of tender translucent blue, ever shifting and widening their shores, till, as the flame-colour sank beneath the horizon, they became more frequent, and touched with a purer light, as if they had caught some reflection from heaven beyond.

Once Madcap lifted her pale face to the sky, but never once looked back . . . her life was upheaved, and amidst its ruins she saw only the figure that stalked before her, upstanding yet, but at any moment in direst need of her support.

On the threshold of the Red Hall she paused, and turned her head, perhaps feeling a faint pang that her eyes sought in vain for Lord Lovel. And then the door closed behind her, and the hardest lesson of her life was before her to unriddle.

## CHAPTER VI.

*'Cauld and eerie were the words
They twa had them between.'*

AN hour after sunset Frank Lovel walked in his woods, in which there reigned the profound, even awful stillness that affects some persons in the same way as the strange, shuddering fear of the sea that is shared by nearly all animals.

He had no such fear, but his nerves were unstrung, and often he looked behind, as if expecting to see one whose footfall he could not hear, and there was no joy in the glance that scanned each avenue, glade, and dell, though he knew that they had come back to him as his own inheritance, free of shame, that day.

But he saw only the girlish figure supporting the father that she loved, and whom his words had slain; and he stood still to smite his brow with his clenched fist, and curse himself that he had not lied to him, and would have cursed himself again for having yielded to the temptation to revisit Lovel, when suddenly the remembrance of Madcap's kiss fell upon him, and, with an eerie sense of her mother near him, he paused before the very trees by which she had unconsciously foretold to him his future.

They had been young chestnuts then, and in autumn had elected to burst out into an entire new suit of leaves and flowers, and, struck by the sight, she had said to him, 'Frank, don't those trees make you think of a human life in more ways than one? Of a life that has been happy, and all at once trouble came to it, and stripped it of everything, just as the chaffers came in spring, and destroyed the leaves of these trees, leaving them bare, when those around were beautiful and happy; but now, in autumn, just when all the others are sober and dull, these have their youth renewed, just as that life might be even more beautiful and happy in its autumn than its spring.'

'But there are some lives, as there are certain trees, that cannot be so renewed,' Frank had said sadly; 'once stripped of happiness, the heart never stirs in them again; and, after all, these seem to me the grandest trees, the noblest hearts.'

'No!' Madcap had cried; 'that which has once loved for love's sake, been happy for another's sake, may have thought it has lost all, but yet carries it in itself to produce as perfect fruit as any that has gone before, and its second youth is possible, as to that tree which has so boldly reversed the edict of fate.'

But Frank had shaken his head . . . there could be no second Madcap to him in the world; or so he thought then, and lo! as magically as the trees had been restored, so to him in middle age had his youth been renewed in the message she had left him— the sweetest message that a woman could, and that might have fulfilled itself in his perfect happiness had not Mr. Eyre's crime seemed to for ever separate his daughter and his friend.

'Oh, Madcap! Poor murdered Madcap!'

he said aloud, his loathing for the hand that had so mercilessly slain her rising up with all its old fierceness, and driving out pity for the stricken man who yet persisted in his lie of innocence to the end.

What could have been his motive? Frank wondered for the thousandth time. Not jealousy, for he had no cause; not fear of Hester, for his was not a nature to know fear; not lack of love, for no woman was ever so faithfully, jealously, fondly loved; nor could madness have prompted the deed, for, if eccentric, Mr. Eyre had given no signs of an unsettled reason, and during the trial of Hester Clarke that ensued he gave each day convincing proofs of the power and undimmed brilliancy of his mind.

And this last was the most damning blot of all—that, knowing himself guilty, he should deliberately accuse, and bend all his energies to hang, the woman whose only sin had been that she had loved him, and had wearied him. Strange, that if he must kill one of the two who had so profoundly loved him, he had not killed Hester, and lived his life out happily enough with Madcap; for surely conscience was dead in the man who could not only successfully act a living lie, but as between man and man forfeit his honour by swearing falsely.

And upon his young daughter the shame, the sin, the condemnation must fall; and Frank's heart grew cold as he recalled the look on Madcap's face when, in possession of the truth that he had withheld from her, she lifted her eyes to his, and he saw the awful change in her that one short hour had worked.

How long ago was it that she had flouted him, that she had smiled at him, that she had stooped with love in her eyes, and kissed him? How long since she had looked at him with blazing eyes and called him an assassin? And now she was alone, able to sit down with folded hands and see broken at her feet the religion, the love of years . . . but no—no! Not to sit above them, but to gather up those poor remains, to hug them to her breast, to warm them at her heart, and in her father's ruin and dishonour to cling to him more faithfully than in the days of his pride!

For her sake, perhaps, Mr. Eyre, once convinced of how futile was his attitude of denial, would submit to his fate, and beyond the few immediately concerned, no one would be the wiser as to the real truth concerning Mrs. Eyre's death; but if he persisted in his perjury, if he again accused Hester Clarke, and forced into the witness-box the man who had by word of mouth received confession of the murder, as Hester Clarke had been actually the witness of it, then nothing could save him from the public obloquy and disgrace that he had deliberately drawn on himself.

'Poor little sweetheart—little child!' he said aloud, as he reached the cowslip-gate, only to find that some one was leaning over it—a somebody who turned to stare at him with something more than the usual savage disgust with which the Englishman resents an intrusion on his privacy.

'This is not common property,' said Gordon brusquely; 'and this gate is used only by visitors to or from the Red Hall.'

His troubled angry eyes took a new expression as they met Lord Lovel's, and a suspicion that had been haunting him all day leaped into jealous life as he scanned the face before him.

'You are here to keep an appointment?' he said, his voice bitter with scorn and pain: 'then I will withdraw, for even trespassers have their rights.'

As Gordon turned, and Frank saw the signs of misery in his face, it was suddenly brought home to him how great a wrong he had done this young man, in suffering him to be brought up in, and grow to, a position from which at any moment he was liable to be ousted. And more than that, alas! for had not propinquity, youth, and natural tastes in common, made Madcap and he one of those ideal pairs whose marriages are said to be registered in heaven? And he had come between them.

'I am no trespasser,' he said; 'and it is better that you should know the truth from me than from Mr. Eyre. I am your cousin, Frank Lovel; but for certain reasons I exchanged name and identity with Major Methuen after his death.'

'And these reasons?' said Gordon, his back to the gate, his eyes on the man who for the moment he saw only as Madcap's lover, not the rightful heir come to cast him out of his kingdom; 'they must be strange ones, since no urgency on the part of Mr. Eyre could force you to reveal them.'

'He sought me as Methuen,' said Frank slowly. ' now he knows me for myself; and whatever my faults may have been, he does not despise me.'

'And you think it honourable to wear one man's name, then quietly resume your own, thereby cheating another out of his inheritance—and more?' said the young man, with a contempt of look that stung like a lash. 'There may be reasons why a man should be ashamed to look another in the face—why he should skulk, and hide, make excuses (each a lie) rather than speak out; but I hope there are few who would steal into an English gentleman's house in his absence and win his daughter's affections on false pretences.'

'Let him keep who is able to win,' said Frank grimly. 'You had your chance, and you missed it. But on Mr. Eyre it depends whether you keep the inheritance I deliberately forfeited in your favour. If he elects to keep silence on the circumstances that led to my banishment, I shall at once leave England, and for ever; but if he insists on raking up the whole dreadful business, I have no choice but to remain, and appear as witness.'

'What business?' said Gordon curtly.

'Has she not told you?' exclaimed Frank.

'I have not seen *Miss Eyre* since about three o'clock this afternoon,' said Gordon, 'when I happened to tell her that I saw you departing in the same train from which I got out. No doubt you had just left her,' added the young man, with a forced sneer; ' and apparently you were in some haste to return.'

'In so much,' said Frank drily, 'that I jumped out of the train as soon as it had cleared the station, and instead of breaking my neck, came off with a smashed arm; and, after all, it had better have been my neck.'

'And you have been carrying it about unset for nearly five hours!' exclaimed Gordon; 'come up to the house—your own house—man, and have it attended to.'

'Presently,' said Frank, 'for I won't go

out of sight of the Hall. There will be trouble there to-night, and worse to-morrow.'

'What is it?' said Gordon, thrusting aside all thought of Madcap as he looked at the pallid face, which bore fewer signs, indeed, of triumph than of intense mental and bodily pain.

'You are bound to know, sooner or later,' said Frank slowly, 'so you had better have the truth now. Mr. Eyre murdered his wife, and believed his crime undetected. By an extraordinary accident, to-day he has seen the only two persons on earth who could have convicted him of it—Hester Clarke and myself.'

'Hester Clarke!' cried Gordon, in horror; 'why, that is the woman whom he suspected—whom he caused to be imprisoned, and nearly hanged on circumstantial evidence!'

'And who would have submitted to be hanged, rather than betray him,' said Frank.

'And the other witness?' exclaimed Gordon.

'Is here,' and Frank touched his breast. 'In Mr. Eyre's brain fever, after the trial, he revealed every incident of the tragedy, went through it in pantomime, and even showed the place in which he had placed the blood-stained knife found by Hester; but I believed these were mere hallucinations, till, on describing them to her (for she had lingered in the place to know the issue of his dangerous illness), I saw such signs in her face as convinced me that she alone knew the real secret of Madcap's death. Bit by bit, I wrung it from her; how she had seen the murder committed by his hand; but because she believed herself instrumental in it, would have died rather than accuse him.

'Together we agreed to go different ways, to leave him to fate, chance, himself; but as quickly as he had strength to move, he set out in pursuit of me. No doubt you have heard the story: how, after long search, he thought he came up with me at Sevastopol, but only to confound me with another man, whose body he brought home, and who was buried in my name. I had been dangerously wounded by Methuen's very side, and when I came to myself, was on board a steamer, sent home as a hopeless invalid, and with my name and personality changed to that of "Methuen." No one in the ship had known either of us by sight; half the officers in my regiment were dead, or had remained to fight; there was not a soul to swear to my real identity; but I had forgotten that in taking Major Methuen's name I had also incurred his responsibilities, and only afterwards remembered that he had a mother to whom he was most deeply attached, and who was, no doubt, watching the papers eagerly for news of him each day.

'I resolved to go to her, to tell her the truth; but on landing I became so ill that the doctors gave me over, and I sent for her—only to be wept over with tears of joy as her *son*. I could not tell her then; but later, when I had turned the corner, I did. At first she would not believe it, declared that the injury to my head had affected my brain, and that she could swear to me as her own child; nor was this idea ever uprooted from her mind, and from then till the time of her death, I made my home with her as her son, and came to love her as if she had really been my mother.

'We travelled constantly, but rarely visited London. At the end of thirteen years, I saw announced the death of Mr. Eyre on board the sailing ship *Arizona*, and I resolved to return to England, and, as a stranger, re-visit Lovel to see Job, and decide whether I would resume the name I had deliberately forfeited. I arrived just in time to hear his last words, and remained long enough to get the news that Mr. Eyre was safe, and would soon return; but between the two events I had seen Madcap.'

Gordon lifted his head, and looked at the man who had so bitterly wronged him, yet had so bitterly suffered. And in his jealous, passionate heart began to stir something of the old hero-worship that had made his dead cousin a living example to his own life.

'It was here that I saw her, and I thought it was her mother's spirit that came tripping over the cowslip-heads to meet me, for I believed Mrs. Eyre's infant to be dead, and here was her living image, just as lovely, as sweet, as dear; and she spoke to me, she was kind to me, and I fell in love with her. I had never ceased to love her mother, and this new love was but a continuation of the old. I knew the last to be as hopeless as the first; that, face to face with Mr. Eyre, I could not have hidden my knowledge of his crime, and rather than accuse him, I again left England, resolved never to return. But Mrs. Methuen's increasing illness brought us back to London, and though I shunned my fellow-men, accident one evening brought me face to face with him. He recognised me on the spot, and thenceforth pursued me. I was tied to the house where my adopted mother lay dying, and somehow managed to evade him.

'Meanwhile, I saw you sometimes, and envied you. You were to be Madcap's husband, and report said that she looked at no man but you. My mother died, and was removed to the country for burial, and I was following her the next day, when, driving in opposite directions, I met Madcap.'

He paused, then said abruptly:

'I don't know why I am telling you all this, but that I want you to know I have not acted in as underhand a way as you supposed. I followed her to the rose-show; we spoke, and parted. I never expected to see her again; and, having buried my mother, came straight here yesterday. To my surprise, I found Hester Clarke in the village, bent on one of those visits to Dody's grave that were impossible when Mr. Eyre was at home. Never was there a more fatal one than this, for without her evidence Mr. Eyre might have feigned to believe me a madman; but they have met, and he has forced from her every detail of the murder.'

'Whose murder?' said the voice of Doune close behind them, and the two men turned to see a younger image of Mr. Eyre, pale, and with flashing eyes that looked from one to the other in angry question. 'I am no eaves-dropper,' he added, before either could speak, 'and always go this way to the Red Hall. But I could not help hearing certain words that demand an explanation. You and I' (he turned to Gordon) 'always knew the accusations against the dear old father

—but it will be curious if a *stranger* proves them true.'

He got no answer, only averted looks, for here was a difficulty for which neither was prepared. Perhaps Gordon knew best how the long alienation between father and son had been gradually broken down, till only love and trust lay between them; but Frank remembered the stubborn childish hate that had vexed the boy's mother, and saw new misery for Mr. Eyre ahead.

'Are you both *dumb?*' cried the young man fiercely; 'then I will get the truth from my father!' and he flung the gate open, and crossed the meadow.

## CHAPTER VII.

*' Unfit to live or die—O marble heart!
After him fellow! drag him to the block.'*

MR. EYRE had locked himself in his study on his return, and though he had not tasted food since his arrival at noon, none durst disturb him—not even Madcap, who forced herself to eat, knowing the work that lay before her.

But later she heard sounds like blows on the locked door, and ran out to see Doune standing pale and grim as fate waiting for admittance; and even as she would have drawn him back, the bolts revolved, and Mr. Eyre faced them, gaunt and terrible; though while he beckoned the son in, he shut the daughter out.

'Father,' said Doune, as they stood face to face, 'did you kill my mother?'

'So they say,' said Mr. Eyre; 'for there are two witnesses—the one who *saw* it, and the one to whom I confessed it. Yet I swear that I am innocent of the deed, and they are either mad or conspirators who accuse me.'

'Who are your accusers?' said Doune.

Something in his son's voice smote him like a blow; but Mr. Eyre's face only hardened as he said:

'You will find both in the village: their names are Hester Clarke and Frank Lovel.'

'Frank Lovel!' exclaimed Doune, starting violently. 'He is dead—or was your bringing of his body home a—a——'

'Call it a lie, if you will.' said Mr. Eyre coldly, ' and believe everything against me that is possible. To-night I am arranging my affairs; to-morrow morning I send to Busby, as the nearest magistrate, and surrender myself at Marmiton Gaol. Either those who have falsely accused me shall come forward to bear witness against me, or I will reckon them the basest traitors that ever disgraced God's earth. Against the traitors of my own household I cannot guard. Go to your sister—if she is not abroad with her lover. I have work to do, and must be alone to-night.'

For a moment the eyes of father and son met as antagonists; then Doune, without a word, turned and went out.

Madcap was waiting, but only by the

light she held made herself known as she followed him to the room where hung that picture of his mother to which he had turned in his every childish and boyish trouble, and in whose lineaments now he seemed to trace a shadow of the awful fate that had overtaken her.

'Mother—*mother!*' he said aloud; then saw Madcap standing there, pale, and with down-bent head, yet with a vigour in her attitude that did not betoken despair.

'So it is true,' he said slowly, 'and all these years he has been a living and acting *lie;* and I was right when, as a child, I hated him for driving me from her—for he was jealous, and he killed her.'

He dashed one hand across his eyes, shuddering violently, and Madcap did not dare to approach him till the paroxysm was past; then stole gently to his side, and said:

'It is true that he killed her—but he does not know it.'

Doune laughed, and never had father and son shown a more remarkable resemblance to each other than in that moment. The very extravagance of gesture and voice were identical; yet Madcap's heart rose, rather than sank, as she saw each token of Mr. Eyre's mental trouble reproduced in her brother.

'He killed her, and he does not know it!' said the young man, his haggard eyes seeking that beloved mother-face; 'you talk madness... Oh, unnatural wretch!' he cried, striking his foot against the floor; 'and she loved him—she died in his arms; she could scarcely spare a look even for her children! And with that awful knowledge in his heart, with her blood upon his hand, he could seem to love, to cherish us——'

'And he *did*,' said Madcap firmly.

'What! is it all blotted out in your mind, how he has had no thought—no care for himself all these years, but only for *us*? And now that he needs us most, shall we repay him with ingratitude? Do not judge him to-night, or by the morning you may be sorry.'

Doune drew back, and looked at her with the first unkind glance he had given her in his life.

'Women have strange minds,' he said harshly; 'they will cling to and fawn on the hand that destroys them; but to a man, a fact is a fact, to-morrow is not to-day. Does he mean to escape to-night?' he added, turning to her suddenly; 'for that would be the most cowardly act of all; and you would be a criminal to assist him, since his sole act of grace would be to confess, and clear the woman he accused.'

'He will not escape,' said Madcap coldly, but with her heart beating fast. 'Are you going to stay here to *watch* him?' she added, with a gibe in her voice that brought the blood to his pale cheek.

'Not I; it would suffocate me to remain under the same roof with him. No doubt I can find a lodging in the woods——' He paused as if struck by a sudden thought; then said—'My father spoke of you as probably abroad with a lover. Did he mean Gordon?'

'No,' said Madcap, as naturally as if she had said 'Yes.'

'The father first, the sister next,' said Doune; 'is there anyone left on earth to trust?'

'There is Nanciebel,' said Madcap.

Sorely tried as she was, the old invincible spirit looked out of her eyes, and a hidden source of happiness within dared to breathe softly, while a secret hope of saving her father lent strength to go through with her work to the end.

For a moment Doune's face softened, then grew hard as iron.

'I love her,' he said; 'but if I had known yesterday what I know to-day, I would not have asked her to be my wife. A felon's son may inherit more than physical traits, and a young girl's life may not be safe with him.'

'Has she no courage?' said Madcap, with a scorn instantly repented of, as she saw how intense his suffering was. 'My dear,' she said, putting her arms round him, 'go home to Gordon. By the morning I may have something to tell you that will clear our father. Or'—her voice sank lower—'there may be fresh misfortunes that I prefer to face alone.'

'You always loved him best,' said Doune jealously, as he turned away, 'just as *she* did——'

'But you have your Nanciebel,' she said softly, as if the thought of loving, and being loved, had for a moment thrust her father from her mind.

'And you have your lover,' he said bitterly. 'I don't know his name.

'His name is Lord Lovel,' she said proudly.

'The man who has masqueraded so long as Major Methuen; the man I saw just now in Lovel woods talking with Gordon?'

'Yes,' said Madcap; 'he will not run away any more—he means to stay.'

'Madcap!' cried the young man, seizing her hand, 'what does all this mean? You admit yourself to be the dupe of a madman whom you have become acquainted with in some clandestine manner, and you deliberately tell me in one and the same breath that our father is at once guilty and innocent.'

'If Frank Lovel is mad, then I am mad too,' said Madcap; 'but to-morrow morning——' she paused, and thought of those desperate issues of the night to which she was committed, and through which none might help her—'perhaps by to-morrow light will have come . . . and if you ever prayed for us, Doune—for father and me—you will pray for us to-night.'

But there was less of prayer than of cursing in Doune's heart as he loosed his sister's hand and strode away.

## CHAPTER VIII.

'*I had happier died by thee,
Than lived on as Lady Leigh.*'

DUSK faded into darkness before Madcap moved from where Doune had left her; then she stole to the library door, but a profound silence reigned within, and she went softly out to the courtyard to see if her father had kindled lights.

But the shutters were closed, and only the stars gave a clue to the figure that crouched close against the window, and to which Madcap drew closer, till she touched it, but got no answer save a shudder of fear, as if the touch of a policeman, not a friend, were on its arm.

'You are Hester Clarke,' said Madcap below her breath, and lifted a fold of the cloak that hid the woman's face; then said, 'Come with me,' in a voice there was no resisting, even if her hand had not drawn the intruder with her towards the stone steps that led to the nursery.

What memories thronged round Hester as she ascended them . . . yet, as one who walked in a dream, she followed the girl into the room where Dody had died on her knees, and she had been dragged away as the murderer of his mother.

A lamp burned dimly—by its light the two looked at each other; then Hester sank to her knees, and with trembling, kissed the girl's hand.

'Why do you do that?' said Madcap; 'for you have done no wrong. You spoke this afternoon of your sin, your weakness; but to me it seems that you have behaved nobly.'

Lower the woman's head sank till her face was hidden, and only a keen ear could have caught the words, ' You don't know . . . and I can't find words to tell you.'

'Tell me,' whispered Madcap, with a chill foreboding that pierced even her absorption in what lay before her, yet with her eyes fixed on the windows of the opposite wing.

I don't know how the words struggled out, how the confession was made . . . but the worst was over, when Madcap knelt, and lifted the dark head to her breast, and heard the rest through half-broken sobs, as Hester leaned against her.

'It was just so that *she* put her arms round me ... once in the copse when she only knew me as a stranger, and in trouble, and again when she knew nothing but ill of me ... it was the very day she died, and my heart was full of envy and bitterness when we met ... I meant to steal her child when she was safely over her trouble; and in this very room I told your father that he should suffer for his sins through *her*. And he thought that I meant to kill her; and he never knew how, half an hour later, she and I came face to face, and I don't know which of us spoke first ... but she kissed me, and I swore to myself then, that no matter what came to me, I would never harm her, nor anyone that she loved. Perhaps some foreboding touched her, though she seemed so happy, for she said when we parted, "I am glad that I have understood you—at last;" and once she looked back, and there was something so solemn and sweet in her eyes, that after she had gone, I cried, with a presentiment that I should never see her again.'

Hester paused, and shivered through and through.

'But I saw her once more . . . I could not let well alone, and I stole here late at night to see Dody . . . he was my one joy on earth, my idol, and I knew him to be ill, though Josephine hid it from your mother; and though it tore my heart in two, I resolved that night to go away, and not even let my shadow come between your father and that lovely, sweet soul. . .'

'Perhaps you can't understand it,' she went on, lifting her head, 'that a woman should love a young child so . . . but perhaps it is *because* he is so young, because his ways are so dear, and that every passionate instinct of protection is roused by him in one's breast, that one loves him so... Do you think a mother bears with a grown-up child's ingratitude because she loves him as he is? No! but because she remembers him as he was, and his words and looks come back to her... and Dody was the living image of what my own child might have been...'

She drew a little away from Madcap as she spoke, but the girl did not shrink; it seemed to her that nothing new could come to her now... since yesterday she had touched every note of the whole gamut of human joy and sorrow.

'I had barely time to kiss him,' resumed Hester, forcing herself to the end of her narration, 'when steps approached from outside, and I had just time to hide myself before Lord Lovel came in. He approached Dody's bed, but made no search for me, and went through to the day nursery, being met there by Josephine. Here was my opportunity; I kissed my dear love and stole away, but a light in his mother's room seemed to beckon me, and I crossed the courtyard meaning only to look up, and bespeak her a blessing before I went.

'My foot struck against something hard as I stood outside the library window; I put out my hand, and found it was a ladder, and some mad impulse made me climb it. You know the rest . . . would to God he had killed me, not her, that night!'

'No,' said Madcap, in a low voice, 'for if he had killed *you*, it would have been murder—he would have done it with intention; but with my mother——' she checked herself suddenly, then said:

'I have work to do to-night, and you must help me. I meant to go through with it alone, but as you saved him once, so you shall help to save him again: only differently, for then you will know that in heart and spirit he is—innocent.'

Both were standing now, and Madcap saw how a kind of incredulous fear spread over Hester's face; then the woman stooped, and humbly kissed her hand.

'Set me what work you will,' she said; 'the harder the better.'

'Listen,' said Madcap. 'It is now ten o'clock, and I will tell the servants (there are only three; the others are in town) to shut up the house and go to bed. No one will come here, and I will bring you food, and then—then——'

The girl did not finish her sentence as she ran out, and Hester stood immovable for awhile, then crossed the room to where Dody's little bed had once stood, and with a sob kneeled down beside the empty space, and covered her face with her hands.

Was her sin never to be blotted out? was it to go on fulfilling itself in endless cycles of suffering that involved the innocent more cruelly than the guilty?

She was kneeling there still when Madcap returned, and the sound of her own weeping made inaudible those light steps that presently stopped beside her.

'Come and eat,' said the girl, laying a gentle hand on the still beautiful head, now abased to the very dust.

Hester rose at once, and went to the table, set out with bread and meat and wine.

When she had forced herself to eat and drink, she said to Madcap, who was watching the opposite wing:

'I am ready.'

Madcap put out her hand, and without a word led her down the stone steps into the courtyard.

'We must be quick,' she said, 'for he may go upstairs at any moment;' and hand in hand the two ran to a tool-house that was dark as pitch, but from which Madcap presently issued, staggering under the weight she bore.

It was the ladder that first Hester had climbed, then Digges, lastly Mr. Eyre; and it felt like lead to Hester as she lifted one end up, and with an instinctive knowledge of Madcap's purpose, led the way.

When it was firmly placed—but so quietly that none within could have heard a sound, the girl drew the woman aside, and said:

'I am asking you something hard—but you said the harder the better; and it is for *his* sake; and if you should feel the cold out here, you will know there is some one colder still within. . .'

'What shall I do?' said Hester, in a whisper.

'You will watch my mother's window—the room which is still my father's bedchamber. The moment you see a light within, you will climb the ladder and watch. No matter what happens, you must not cry out, or speak. You must not interfere . . . if he should kill me, you will steal away as you did before, and keep his secret; but by the morning' (she touched Hester's hand) 'I think that to both of us light will have come.'

## CHAPTER IX.

*'Said I not that all God sends is good? Only generally it is not until the morning that we see why He denied us something in the evening.'*

*Gesta Romanorum.*

HOW do inspirations, desperate resolves, enter a human soul? Are they kindled by sheer agony, longing, or prayer? But to Madcap a divine message seemed to have come, when at midnight she went with trembling limbs to the room which was to be the scene of her desperate experiment.

In the study below, Mr. Eyre worked swiftly and monotonously through the business that most concerned him and his, until all was in order, and his man of business, or his executor—nay, his daughter even—could find no difficulty in fulfilling his last wishes and administering his estate.

His wife's love-letters to him were duly secured in his breast; the old Army-Guide lay open on the table, with the name 'Methuen' scored out, and 'Lovel' marked with red ink in its place; but among the sealed letters lay one with neither seal nor enclosure, though it was addressed to 'Miss Eyre.'

The confusion of his mind had by now subsided, leaving only a fixed belief in Hester's guilt, in Frank's confirmed madness, and Madcap's profound deceit; while of Doune he scarcely thought at all.

But with pen in hand, ready to write

down scathing words of reproach (for he meant to give himself up to justice on the morrow, and force his accusers to appear before him), he suddenly fell into a sound sleep or stupor, his eyes fixed on the unsullied page, his hand rigid, his whole body immovable, as if struck to stone by a wizard's wand.

For half an hour he sat thus. Then, still in that catalyptic trance, laid down the pen, stretched his hand to the light, which he lifted; then with even steps crossed the room to the private stair communicating with his bedroom.

Two women, who had grown cold with watching, even in the midst of summer heat, saw the zigzag light of the candle showing on the corkscrew staircase, heard the steps ascend, then saw Mr. Eyre enter, the light wavering over his fixed face and wide-opened eyes — O heavens! *in his sleep?* Almost aloud Madcap prayed it, as at sight of the white figure seated in his wife's chair he stopped short, then advanced with violence towards her, feeling in his breast as for a weapon; then, turning as by remembered instinct to the cabinet near, opened a drawer, in imagination snatched a knife, and stabbed at her, once, twice, exclaiming 'Die! *die!*' in a voice of fury. Then, making as though he replaced the weapon, turned, and went down the staircase, holding the light steadily, and with no sign of either hurry or discomposure on his features.

She followed him down, love's work being not completed yet, and saw him seat himself at the table; but when, trembling, she stole nearer, she saw by his wide-open fixed eyes that he was still asleep, though his folded arms rested on the edges of a large book that he had opened and set before him.

Then Madcap kneeled down beside him, knowing that her prayer had been granted, and that love's miracle had saved him . . . then sight and sense failed her, and she fell forward with her bright hair veiling her face, as her head sank on his knee.

\* \* \* \* \*

Hester Clarke had entered with amazement and terror into Madcap's scheme that night, for she went blindfold, and without the clue upon which the girl's hand had so firmly closed.

She had climbed the ladder with fear, and nearly lost her balance on it, when, through the half-open window, she saw the room with everything in it arranged exactly as when she had last seen it, seventeen years ago—the very chair, the very figure seated in it, completed the picture that was graven on her heart.

The jewel-cases lay open on the table, and a lace handkerchief on the smaller one beside Madcap, just as Mrs. Eyre had tossed it down on the diamonds that Josephine's covetous eyes had detected an hour later, and stolen with Digges's knowledge, to her own undoing and his . . . nothing was needed to complete Hester's illusion that she was dreaming, save Mr. Eyre's appearance on the scene; and, icy cold with fear and apprehension, she awaited it.

The night wore on. She put one arm within the stone casement to steady herself the better; but she never once tried to attract the attention of the quiet figure that, seated with its back to her, seemed not to have moved a muscle since she approached.

But all the past fulfilled itself, even to the minutest detail, when Mr. Eyre's light showed on the stair, and in pantomime he repeated each gesture, each blow, she had seen him use when he killed his wife. But to her older eyes (as to Madcap's young ones) a clearer light had come; and as Mr. Eyre disappeared, and the girl followed him, it was borne in upon her how, not by her sin alone, but by her testimony against him, she had committed an irreparable wrong.

All was explained now: his firm belief in her guilt; his pursuit of her, and strenuous endeavours to get her hanged; his search for Lord Lovel; and his hatred for the friend who could hurl a false accusation (as Mr. Eyre believed) against him, then run away, as if too cowardly to even try and substantiate the lie; the inward sense of innocence sustaining him, so that suspicion passed him by unscathed, and he could exclaim, 'This hand is innocent!' . . . ay! as in sooth it was, if it committed automatically a deed from which the will, consent, and controlling power of the mind were absent.

A great wave of love, of pity, swept over Hester's soul as she bowed her head on the casement, and thought of how he must have suffered, of how infinitely more he must suffer yet, when the truth should reach him from his daughter's lips. Perhaps he was learning it below even now; but her heart sank lower and lower, as the minutes passed, and no sign from Madcap came to release her from her post.

Towards dawn a slight stir reached her ear, and the next moment she heard steps rising from the study, and saw the flicker of a light on the wall. She leaned forward with a half-sob of relief, only to shrink back as she saw Mr. Eyre enter, pale as a corpse indeed, but *awake!*

'How could she ever have mistaken him?' she wondered, as, weak and numbed, she cowered down, invisible from within the lamp-lit room, though without, in the clear, strengthening dawn, she might be distinctly seen, and was every moment in danger of discovery.

He set the light down, and for the last time approached the cabinet about which for seventeen years his brain had held some secret knowledge that defied him.

Hester heard him open a drawer, and then followed a long and profound silence, in which, for the last time, the one half of his brain struggled with the other; and as he had wrung the truth from Lord Lovel and Hester that day, so now he thought he forced the lock of that sealed chamber which had defied him, and *saw*. All was apparently clear to him now—the seated figure by the window in Synge Lane that he had *desired* to kill was Hester; the figure that he had actually killed in a fit of madness of which he had no memory was his wife, and he had put the knife back in the cabinet as the woman described ... he remembered now, that the cry for help that night had roused him from a dream of appalling vividness, in which he was in the act of stabbing Hester to the heart, and even woke with a passionate feeling of exultation that he was rid of her, and that his wife's happiness was now secure.

When Parrhasius struggled to depict the supremest agony of which a human being is capable, he *covered* the face of the man he delineated, and only by the attitude of the limbs and hands revealed the intention of his work. Some such awful expression stole slowly over Mr. Eyre's averted head and body, as Hester for a few frozen seconds watched him; then, without a sound, she shrank out of sight and crept down the ladder, whence, regaining Madcap's empty room, she sat down by the window to watch.

## CHAPTER X.

'*It is conscience that preserves the right of the will.*'

MADCAP came out of that long slumber feeling like a soldier who has lain down to sleep at the post of duty, for the room was empty, the fresh morning wind blew in through the open window, and the village clock was striking the hour of nine.

Signs of Mr. Eyre's late presence were visible in the cloak he had wrapped about her, and the pillow he had placed beneath her head; and when a hasty glance round assured her that he had left no letter, she persuaded herself that his absence was but momentary, and going to the foot of the private staircase, she listened for signs of him above. A quick step in the room made her turn, only to start back as at a frightful apparition, for all dishevelled, his hair wet with dew, his gaze wild, and his mien that of a madman, her brother stood before her.

'O God!' he cried, before she could speak, 'that he can breathe—that he can say "*This hand* did the deed,' and yet it does not wither—his tongue is not struck dumb by fire from the heaven to which he sent her! Mother—poor murdered mother!—perhaps you knew it, and forgave him—*him*, inhuman wretch!—whom you loved better than your children. Hearken!' (he seized Madcap's hand in a grip of steel, pouring out his words with such rapidity that it was impossible to check him); 'all night I have wandered in the woods with a hell in my breast, with the hatred of Cain for Abel burning in me against our father. In vain I have sought excuses, have tried to persuade myself the murder was no murder, but an accident, or some hideous mischance; I forced myself to recall his care of me, his tenderness for you: I reviewed the upright life he has led ever since I was old enough to judge between right and wrong, and by morning I had subdued that unnatural hatred, and longed only to be face to face with him, to hear any explanation—any palliation of the crime that might render him less abhorrent to me; and it was with even a faint feeling of hope that I sought him here.'

Madcap strove to speak—to interpose, but Donne's vehement words swept hers aside as straws in a torrent, and she could only wait till, by his violence, he had exhausted himself.

'I found him; God knows what thoughts swelled my heart as I approached him—of our mother, of Dody, of you, of her—for she loves me, Madcap . . . I have caught a timid look now and then . . . and her voice—but I have heard it for the last time——'

'No, no!' cried Madcap, as for the first time he paused, and an expression of despairing tenderness crossed his convulsed features; 'she loves you, and our father is innocent——'

'Innocent!' cried Doune, turning upon her with a frenzied gesture of intolerant contempt. 'He owned the deed—he avowed it without ruth or shame; he offered not one word in condonation, and seemed to forget it was my *mother* to whose murder he so indifferently confessed. Even to my curses——'

'You have cursed him!' cried Madcap, sinking down in terror. 'Oh, you know not what you have done! Father, poor father!' and she moved as though to go in search of him.

'Say rather "*Poor mother!*"' said Doune, in a voice that brought tears to Madcap's eyes, though his own still retained the hard, strained look that so alarmed her. 'Murdered,' he went on rapidly, and gazing before him as at some frightful sight—'her life-blood ebbing away under the arm that clasped Dody and I when we kissed her last; and Frank Lovel's life ruined, and mine too, and *hers* . . . and beyond all these, Hester Clarke and Janet Stork, more victims to his sins; and this is the man we have loved, we have honoured——'

'And whom we may love and honour still,' cried Madcap, swift as light; 'for he committed the murder *in his sleep!*'

For a moment Doune's face worked strangely, and she thought he trembled on the verge of dreadful laughter; but to her joy a more rational expression overspread his features, as he said:

'Is it with such wild hopes as these you buoy yourself up, Madcap? So that's why you are bright, although so pale; and a moment ago I thought you heartless, hateful even, to look so. I think I have been mad;' he passed his hand over his eyes, out of which the wild, strained expression was gradually disappearing; 'but a man's brain might turn for less, and now there's the bitter, black reality to be faced, and lived through to our lives' end. But at least we have one another.'

Involuntarily he held out his arms, and for a moment the brother and sister clung to each other desperately, and not as in their happy, childish days.

Then Doune would have put her aside, but she would not let him go; she forced him to hear her, though, as her story progressed, she had less trouble on that point, till its end saw him standing breathless and white before her, but with the dawn of something like hope overspreading his features.

Then she reminded him of how he had walked constantly in his sleep during those dangerous days of his youth, when brain had overmastered body, and he had slipped towards those shadowy boundaries that divide reason from madness; again she brought to his mind the story of Brandon Eyre, and how, though his guilt was clearly proved, he swore his innocency, and died by his own hand rather than live dishonoured; his grandmother, Lady Sara, afterwards swearing that she could explain it all, though her explanation was never given.

All this Madcap urged on her brother with a swiftness that exceeded even his own vehemence of a few minutes before, and stopped only to leave him confounded at the weight of evidence she brought to establish her marvellous assertion that, in truth, their father was, in all save deed, innocent.

A knock at the door disturbed them before he could speak, and Saunders entered, bearing a letter that at the first glance Madcap saw to be from her father.

The old servant's face was sad as he handed it, and looked from the one face to the other. No one knew better than he that trouble had come to the Red Hall, though he little guessed its extent.

Madcap tore open the letter, and, in Mr. Eyre's firm handwriting, read the following :

'Madcap—child—beloved daughter—by the time you receive this I shall have delivered myself up to justice for the murder of your mother. In heart and hand I am guilty, and will suffer for it in due course. *She* has forgiven me—perhaps in time *you*, who have been the joy of my life, the light of my eyes, my good and (except in one instance) most faithful daughter—you who, in the two darkest hours of my life, have come to me, and perchance love me still, in time may learn to forgive your most unhappy, guilty father,

'EYRE.'

She kissed the letter before she gave it to Doune. She saw how he had scored out 'Miss Eyre' and written 'Madcap' on the envelope instead, and by that mute token knew how he had forgiven her the one deception towards him of her life.

But how, without her help to guide him, had he become convinced of his guilt? had Hester blundered, or, with only vague instructions to guide her, meddled fatally in the business of the night? Forgetful of Doune even, she ran up the secret stair, and into the empty room, now flooded with morning light; then she looked out and saw the ladder against the wall, then opposite to where from the nursery a pale face seemed to beckon her—the face of Hester, not Nan.

Nan, indeed, had knocked outside her young mistress's door for some time without getting any answer, and had then retired to breakfast, she being as ignorant as the other women of what had been going on in the house that night.

Mr. Eyre had always been a master whose habits must be neither questioned nor interfered with; his daughter's, too, were so far like his own, that if she happened to take a walk at daybreak, no one dreamed of supposing her to be drowned, or fished for her in the surrounding ponds and puddles. So that when Madcap crossed the courtyard, it would have seemed the most natural thing in the world (had there been any onlookers) that she should have risen early, and gone over to put flowers in her father's study, already set straight against his unexpected return, though her dress was the tumbled one she had worn throughout that dreadful but most blessed night.

Hester sprang up as the girl entered, and the two pale faces turned to one another.

'You know *now?*' said Madcap, out of breath, and with the hurry of imminent need compelling her to abrupt speech ; ' and so you will come with me, and we will bear witness together for *him*. . . .'

Her voice ceased in a sob as she began to pull off her gown ; then vanished, only to reappear fresh bathed, and dressed in something white as snow, and with an eager look of hope on her face that contrasted forcibly with the pallor and pain stamped on Hester's features.

Then, hand-in-hand, the women went down the steps together, the one lightly, the other heavily, and as if the three-mile walk to Marmiton were beyond her strength.

## CHAPTER XI.

' *Since thunder-stricken . . .*
  *Fixed in the spectral strain and throe*
  *Wherewith it struggled from the blow . . .*'

MEANWHILE an extraordinary scene was being enacted at Marmiton Gaol. At eight o'clock Mr. Eyre had walked in and given himself in custody for the murder of his wife; and before the dreadful confession had properly reached the brain of the Governor, who imagined Mr. Eyre to have suddenly gone mad, named Hester Clarke as witness to the deed, and Lord Lovel as being well acquainted with the fact.

The man was at first stupefied; but Mr. Eyre persisting in his story, and showing no other signs of madness, in less than an hour his brother magistrates were summoned, and a scene of the utmost confusion among them prevailed.

He alone was calm, and asked that no one might be admitted to his cell, *especially his daughter*—and as he named her, the first sign of emotion he had yet shown crossed his features.

To Lord Lovel, who was present, and who vainly implored him to withdraw his self-accusation, he said he was resolved on doing his duty, and hoped Frank would do his, and make Hester Clarke do hers; for that though he had disbelieved their story yesterday, in the night he had become convinced of its truth.

He added that Lord Lovel's knowledge

of it had exiled him, and no doubt was the reason of his acquiescence in the case of mistaken identity, by which Major Methuen had been buried under his name, and many living persons persuaded that Lord Lovel, not the other, had died.

Colonel Busby had for once absolutely collapsed under the shock of a double surprise; for though he had all along been convinced that Mr. Eyre was the real murderer, he had never expected him to confess it. He had been equally convinced that Mr. Eyre was at the bottom of Frank Lovel's death, until the arrival of the former with his friend's body, and certain well-authenticated facts proved the young man to have died in battle, and even the supposition that a mistake of identity had been made, was negatived by the recognition that, from Job downwards, all gave him as he lay in humble state at the Towers.

Yet the man lived—was here to stand forth for the man whom he knew to be a murderer; the man who had stolen his sweetheart, filched his good name, banished him from home and country, yet accepted all these favours without a sign of gratitude in the past, or of recognition to-day.

More than one might have pressed forward to take the hand of the soldierly, bronzed man, who at forty-three was handsomer far than at twenty-five — the last date of his public appearance by Mr. Eyre's side—but that, as usual, the latter fixed all eyes, occupied all but transient thoughts, to the exclusion of every other soul present. The greater part of them thought him mad, for Digges's suicide had practically proved him the murderer, while his wife's possession of the diamonds attested to the reason for the deed.

He was reminded of this, but remarking carelessly:

'She must have stolen them after the discovery of the deed; and he, poor wretch, knew it.' turned as if to seek his cell, when he found himself detained by the clasp of two loving arms, and felt the print of a warm kiss upon his hand.

He looked down, and saw his daughter; beyond her, Hester Clarke, with a curious mixture of shame and gladness on her weary face.

'There's your other witness,' he said, pointing to her, and with no signs of ruth for the wrongs he had worked her visible in his glance, any more than of gratitude for the splendid part she had acted towards him.

'What do you do here, child?' he said abruptly to Madcap; 'I told them not to admit you; but I suppose a prisoner's word has no weight. And I can better bear to know myself what I am, than to read such knowledge in your eyes.'

The last words were inaudible to all save the girl, who but held that beloved hand the closer, and kissed it yet again as, struggling to speak, she looked up.

Frank never forgot the father and daughter as they looked then... Sure, such a sight might have drawn

'*Iron tears down Pluto's cheek*'—

the girl's transfigured face, with its upward look of glad tidings, as if, indeed, it bore a heavenly message; Mr. Eyre's, stern, rugged, with down-bent gaze, that softened suddenly to profoundest tenderness as with his left hand he pushed her bright hair back, but strove to draw his right from her breast.

'It is stained with blood—your mother's blood,' he said.

But she cried out, as with the voice of an angel:

'You are innocent. Oh, father! you are innocent!'

'Would to God that I were!' he said, with the first sign of human feeling about the deed that he had yet shown.

'It is true,' said Hester, in a low, distinct voice; 'in heart, soul and intention, you are guiltless—in act alone you are guilty, *for the murder was committed in your sleep.*'

Exclamations of incredulity broke from nearly all present. Colonel Busby's being strongly flavoured with contempt; but Mr. Eyre stood rigid, his eyes fixed on Hester as if he would search her very soul—and in it he found the truth.

The mists rolled away. Aided by some curious knowledge from within, her words made all clear to him, and in one flash of light, one moment of time, was thrown open to him that chamber of his brain which for eighteen years had been closed against him. The discovery that he had made in the night, and which had determined him to give himself up to justice, had been but a partial one, and his supposition that he had committed the deed in a moment of madness, and forgotten it, had gone widely far of the truth.

Not guilty! not guilty in *will* of taking that sweet life . . . a look of joy overspread his features.

'Oh, wife! . . . wife! . . .' he murmured inaudibly, and looking straight before him, as if he saw only a lovesome shape that smiled on, and beckoned him to come to her. . . . He passed his hand across his brows, and was his usual self, as he said, 'Yet I am guilty, for the spirit of murder dwelt in me; and even if my hand unconsciously worked the crime, it did but obey the impulse that, in waking moments, had filled my mind—the impulse' (to Hester Clarke) 'to murder you. *I* was the man seen by the tramp in Synge Lane with a weapon in my hand, which I had taken there with a deliberate intention. So that, in heart and hand alike, I am guilty, and will suffer.' He turned once more to his daughter, and said, 'So you do not shrink from me—*she* did not, though I killed her. And now I must leave you.'

'It's a clear case of committal,' said Colonel Busby, with uneasy dignity; 'and as to this ridiculous story about the sleep-walking, there will be time enough to discuss that when the trial comes on.'

'There is time now,' said Madcap, in a voice that commanded attention; and in brief, vigorous words, she detailed the events of the previous day and night, the interview in the wood with Lord Lovel, the subsequent one with Hester in Synge Lane, that still, and in spite of circumstantial evidence, left Mr. Eyre convinced how both witnesses falsely affirmed his guilt.

Admiration succeeded wonder as she related how, partly from an accidental expression used by Hester, and partly from her own observation of her brother's acts when in a state of somnambulism, the idea had come to her that Mr. Eyre had committed the deed in his sleep, and being ignorant of his act, thought he spoke truth when he denied it. Following this idea came one to personate her mother, hoping that her unexpected presence in his room might awaken in him some memory of the fatal night; and by blessed good fortune the stratagem proved successful, for towards morning, *walking in his sleep*, he came up the private stair, and seeing her sitting there, made as though he snatched a weapon, and saying 'Die! die!' stabbed violently at the air, then turned and went downstairs.

Madcap felt a thrill run through her father as she spoke—she knew his thought, how, if a real instead of an imaginary weapon had been in his hand, he might have slain *her* as he slew her mother.

Her lip trembled—her voice refused to continue the narration . . . a sudden sense of cruelty, of disrespect to *him* in this open dissection of his acts, his motives, this baring of their inmost home-life, smote her, and she turned from the eager faces around to hide her head on his breast.

Then Hester's voice took up the tale, and when she had ended by describing what had that morning been witnessed by herself alone, there was not a soul present, save Colonel Busby, who did not reckon Mr. Eyre in *heart* innocent.

'Yet at your own trial, woman,' said Colonel Busby, beginning to strut, 'you *knew* him to be guilty?'

'I did.'

'And you think a judge and jury will accept a story that has probably its origin in the fevered imagination of two weak women? And who is to know, pray, that the—the murderer'—he pointed to Mr. Eyre—' is not in collusion with you both?'

'Poor busybody!' said Mr. Eyre carelessly, 'too futile to be venomous;' and then he took his daughter's face between his hands, looked at her very earnestly, then kissed her once, and went out.

They heard his receding footsteps dwindle gradually into silence—a silence broken by the sharp clang of the cell-door as it shut upon the man who was at last alone with his heart and God.

## CHAPTER XII.

'*O, see for he gangs, an' see for he stands,*
 *The wearie heir o' Linne!*
*O, see for he stands on the cauld causeway,*
 *And nae ane bids him come in!*'

UTTER silence followed Mr. Eyre's departure; even Colonel Busby's uneasy authority could not be exercised upon a man who had himself committed his body to imprisonment, and the others could not discuss the father in presence of his daughter. But Madcap quickly relieved them of that awkwardness, by retiring with Hester, having in a few brief words asked for, and obtained, permission to remain in the prison, and within call of her father, should he send for her.

She had not once looked at Lord Lovel since she entered, yet knew he was there; and her cheek went paler yet, as a step on the flagged passage followed hers, and on entering the room to which the Governor himself showed her, she looked round only to see Frank in the act of closing the door upon herself and him.

She neither glanced up nor drew breath as he approached; all the spirit, the vigour that had animated her since she had risen elastic from the awful blow of yesterday, now deserted her, and pale and drooping as a beaten-down lily she stood, as Frank came nearer and stood beside her.

'Can you forgive me?' he said, so deeply moved that he could scarcely speak; 'for it is all my fault, my doing. If I had only possessed enough strength of will to keep away from Lovel—or even if I had not returned a second time and gone to the wood, he might have lived and died ignorant of the truth.'

She half looked up then, and saw that he carried his right arm in a sling; but she scarcely noticed it, her mind was so engulfed in thoughts of the wrongs he had so patiently endured, not only at her father's hands, but her own.

Could she forgive him—this idol of her childhood; this more than hero of her youth; this man who had laid his inheritance down, for a lesser than he to take, and gone forth a homeless wanderer, that he might save his friend—the friend who met him with insult, ay, and blows, and whose daughter was so much his own child that she had not scrupled to fling many a bitter gibe and taunt at him?

In one lightning moment she saw all the beauty, the unselfishness of this life that had elected

> 'To suffer and be strong,'

at the cost of happiness. Memory upon memory flashed its light upon him, in the midst of which he stood out apart and alone, something better, brighter, nobler than man or angel had ever shone in her eyes or dreams yet, and she *saw* him as he was.

She saw him acting the part of son, of his own free will giving up his days, submitting to the restraints of hourly avoidance of Mr. Eyre, to soothe the dying pillow of a poor bedridden woman who first loved and clung to him for his likeness to her dead son, then loved him for himself, but by her very affection imposed on him an almost intolerable existence ... and this was the man who had asked the girl only to *trust* him; and had she indeed given so poor a thing as love without faith, to such an one as might well have been

'Aslauga's pure and faithful knight'? ...

She covered her face with both hands; and he, thinking that only an unwilling sense of benefits conferred checked the anger she longed to express (for had she not chosen between them, and chosen her father?), cried out:

'Blame me, Madcap—curse me even, if you will; for whatever I may have done for duty, I have more than undone for love.'

'Oh, sweet fault!' she thought, as lower she bent her head, and said very low:

'You are *sorry* that you came back?'

Her voice startled him with its gentleness . . . once more he lived again that moment of perfect happiness in the wood . . . that moment which God Himself could not take away from him, for it had been his own.

'No, I am not sorry,' he said, and at the passion in his voice Madcap trembled. 'Come what may—cling to your father, and hate me as you will—you have loved me, Madcap, and you have kissed me.'

He could not see the red that mounted to her very brow—he thought her attitude one of aversion to him; and this shrinking in one who had but lately shown such splendid courage astonished him, and brought her nearer to that elder Madcap, who had lacked the strength of will and power of intellect possessed by her daughter.

'I am not sorry,' he repeated more calmly; 'it is you who are sorry—you who will never cease to reproach me for robbing you of your father.'

'How have you done that?' she said, startled; 'they cannot punish him for what he is really guiltless of; and to-morrow—to-day, even—he will come home with me to the Red Hall.'

But Frank stood silent; he knew Mr. Eyre even better than his daughter did, and he foresaw but one ending to the last act of the tragedy that had already destroyed four lives.

But even the thought of her father could not put by her answer to his question, 'Could she forgive him?' . . . perhaps at last her silence answered him, as slowly, and with lips that quivered like those of a child who comes to beg forgiveness, she approached him, and, taking his hand, pressed those trembling lips upon it, then, white and wan, looked up in his face.

Yet never in her most blooming hour had she looked to Frank as now, with those eyes of love, so lovely, so sweet, so true, showing like glimpses of heaven to the man who had summoned such a glance from her heart thither.

For all that he had suffered, all that he had done, he was repaid now. All was washed out, all was forgotten, as they stood gazing at each other; then,

'Madcap!' he said, in a whisper that was yet a sob of joy; but something in her look kept him back, and he only lifted her hands to his breast, and kissed them there.

'You have forgiven me,' she said; 'and now we will only think of father—and Donne. He is quieter now, but some one should be with him. Will you go to him, and tell him that I shall stay here all day, and perhaps all night, within call of father?'

'I will go,' he said, 'and I will come back to you.'

At the door he paused; her eyes were following him, her lips moved as though they uttered words of tenderness that welled up from the heart; he stretched his arms to her, would have returned, but she waved him back; then, as the door closed on him, took shame to herself that in this hour, when alone her father drank his bitter cup, she could find one drop of sweetness in her own.

## CHAPTER XIII.

*'A being of higher faculties requires more to make him happy than one of an inferior type.'*

TEN o'clock found Doune in his father's library, pacing it with restless steps, and but little less disordered than he had appeared to Madcap after his conversation with Mr. Eyre.

In manner he was calmer, but his mind had passed into a more dangerous state, and was now receiving impressions that it would be well-nigh impossible to efface.

Alone he had weighed every word of Madcap's story, and implicitly believed it;

nor had the idea crossed his mind that Mr. Eyre had deliberately simulated the part of a sleep-walker, in order still longer to conceal his crime. He accepted the literal truth, and knew his mother to have been less murdered than the victim of a fatal accident.

But the irresponsibility of the act at once appalled and unnerved him; more than once he looked down at his own hand in doubt and terror, feeling an impulse to strike it off before it, too, should have worked some unnatural deed. A perception of a dual existence, inherited from his father, and in which he moved and even acted without volition, shuddered through his mind, and made his flesh recoil as against itself.

A rooted conviction seized him that his father's fate must inevitably be his own, that his future was inextricably entangled in the guilt of Mr. Eyre's past; their very resemblance to each other in appearance, brain, pursuits, and habits, and of which he had formerly been so proud, now became hateful to him, and the mere chance reflection of himself in a mirror gave him a physical sensation of self-loathing.

He had been too deeply struck by the blow Mr. Eyre's confession had given him to rally for more than a moment under the comparative relief of Madcap's revelation. The fact remained that his mother (that mother who had been the idol of his early childhood, and when lost, so passionately mourned for and remembered, that she was yet the central living figure in all the boy's thoughts and life) had been murdered, and by his father's hand.

That vivid image could never be effaced;

and pity, love, hopeless longing to call back the life that in its joy had made others precious, swelled his heart to bursting, yet could not bring one tear of relief to eyes stern as his father's own, but glazed, as if beyond all outer thought. One sight alone had power to compel and fix his attention.

Was it to such an end that Mr. Eyre's love had pointed, when he took that lovely young life in his hand, and, all ductile as it was, fashioned it to his will? Could he have foreseen that end, would he not have passed it by, to wither perchance from lack of his love, but escaping the violence of a passion which uprooted, when most it should have cherished it?

All the circumstances of her death, as seen from a child's standpoint, crowded thickly on his mind, and brought a new stab, a fresh pang, with each. Even his sister was involved in it, for the knife that pierced the mother must barely have escaped the unborn babe; and, but for a miracle, the two Madcaps must have been slain by one hand. And should he, with that fatal inheritance of his father's person and brain, with even his peculiar idiosyncrasy stamped upon him, take a young innocent soul to himself, and ask it to share a lifelong companionship with one who at any moment might, in irresponsible mistake of his object, wreak the whole force of his hatred, instead of his love, upon her?

Should he bring home this gentle creature (this sunbeam that had not so much played on his eyes, as touched his heart when they first met), to love, make happy, and some day stab to the heart? or should he bring up children only to see the curse fulfilled that he had fortuitously escaped, to see the taint appear that Lady Sara had so deeply rooted in the family some hundred years ago, and that had taken the mark of dishonour in Brandon Eyre?

Never! on this point duty was clear, and heart and will ratified it. If across the gulf that rolled between them he met Nanciebel's suddenly grown tender look, and seemed to see the timid, eager hands outstretched to him, he shut his eyes to their beckoning, and thanked God that hitherto he had tasted so little of love's sweets, that he would be the better able now to endure his unbroken fast of them.

Doubt as to his course had never for a moment occupied his mind; but he had waited till the confusion of it subsided, before he sat down to write that letter to Nanciebel which should end, ere they had well begun, any passages of love between them.

He possessed all his father's decision in thought and act (though fortunately he lacked that inflexibility of will which had more than once blinded Mr. Eyre to consequences, and brought upon him signal disaster), and did not hesitate when presently he took pen in hand to write the first love-letter of his life.

No sense of compassion, of identification with his father's situation, distracted his thoughts from *her* at that moment. There is a strength, a vitality in the selfishness of the young, that makes no excuse as it sweeps all before it, and in the writing of that letter he forgot all on earth save himself and her.

No matter what he said . . . are not such letters scored as in marble on many a young girl's heart—ay, and on many a man's also—and never quite obliterated save by death? There is not much art in such productions, they are seldom read over by the owner of the hand that sets them down, seldomer still does a tear blot their irregular lines, and the hand that folds and addresses them is usually steady.

\* \* \* \* \*

That letter was placed in Nanciebel's hand late on the evening of the same day.

Her packing over, her every arrangement made to start for Lovel early on the following day, she was sitting alone, with shy thoughts that hovered around Doune, yet refused to gaze full-front at the happiness that she knew awaited her.

Love had grown apace with her since that first shock of dread at the thought of leaving him had opened her eyes . . . nay, it had grown even since yesterday, when he had departed for Lovel, without any formal farewell to her, being so sure of seeing her again so soon . . . but was he so impatient already, that he must *write* the words down that had been so much sweeter in the uttering and the hearing? For a little while she sat with the letter in her hand, less as a child who holds some sweet morsel that it longs to taste, yet fears to have its delight too quickly over, than as one who looks beyond it, and sees something so infinitely better as to make comparatively valueless what holds in its grasp.

Yet she kissed the seal before, at last, she broke it, perhaps with some flitting thought that eagerly expectant lovers were not usually so much masters of themselves as to remember sealing-wax; and then, with a long sigh of throbbing joy, the girl kneeled down by the window in the fast-waning light, and read her love-letter.

It was short—she needed not to turn the page; and her poor fingers stiffened over it as she read, so that five minutes later she found herself still staring at a blank page dimly outlined on the darkness, though memory painted in letters of fire the words written upon it.

The words that she had a hundred times checked upon his lips would never now be spoken. '*An obstacle had risen between them that neither time nor Heaven could remove.*' He hinted no more of vain love for her in the future, than he spoke of hopeful love in the past, nor did he imply that he had possession of her heart; yet soul spoke to soul through the stern lines, pitiless as fate, that cut their lives asunder.

She wronged him by no thought of a frivolous pretext, for she had not made him her chief study during the past months without learning his character better perhaps than he knew it himself; and no question of the immutability of his decree crossed her mind as, on the very threshold of her greatest happiness, she found herself rudely thrust back, and set outside it.

So we must leave her . . . so through the long hours of the night must she wrestle with such agony as only the very young and the very strong have power to endure . . . and in the whole wide world she was homeless, and alone.

## CHAPTER XIV.

'*Open the gates,
And let him come in;
He is my brother Huntley,
He'll do him nae harm.*'

ALL that day, none might disturb Mr. Eyre, none dare seek to cross the threshold across which he sat, resolute to shut out by force any who should approach him; but towards evening, those who hearkened heard a slight stir within, and it was Madcap's hand that dared to turn the key and enter.

He was sitting on the pallet that had been successively occupied by Janet Stork as prisoner for the murder of his child, and by Hester Clarke when on trial for the murder of his wife.

There was death in the face he turned on his daughter, and a burning fever scorched the arm that she twined about his neck as she kneeled beside him, and leant her head against his shoulder.

But he unlocked it, and folded both little hands beneath her chin, looking earnestly at her; then said:

'So have I seen you a thousand times asleep — the little golden head drooped forward, and

'"Thy tinny hands on thy wee breast"—

so perhaps has *she*; and when we meet, my one fault in her eyes, that I did not love her children, will be gone. Where's Doune?' he added abruptly; 'the boy took it badly —he should have been the girl, and you the man, for you are made of sterner stuff than he.'

'He is calmer now,' said Madcap, in a low voice, 'for he knows the *truth*.'

'He won't forgive me, for he loved his mother best,' said Mr. Eyre; 'and you'— he still held her from him, and looked at her keenly—'is there no one whom you too love *best*?'

A faint colour overspread her pale face, but her eyes did not falter as she said:

'You were first with my mother, you are first with her child. When you came to the wood, I had just made my choice between Frank Lovel and you; and I had chosen you.'

'You would have done the same if you had known then, what you know now, of his conduct and mine?'

'Yes.'

'Yet you deceived me, child. Wretch as I am, I can yet feel the sting of that.'

'Oh, *father!*' she said; then, quickly, for there was so little to tell, told him all. Perhaps her looks spoke more eloquently than words, and silence best of all, when her head sank forward and she ceased to speak.

'There's no wilful deceit in this,' said Mr. Eyre; 'and so you love him, child; and he has his reward. He lost one Madcap, only to find another; and I lose you, only to find *her.*'

'To find her?' said the girl, trembling. 'Oh no! You would not leave me here alone.'

'Your mother and I have been long apart, child,' he said; 'and I'm in haste to join her. If the law is as swift as it is usually slow, I shall not be impatient long.'

'Father!' cried the girl, shrinking back

in terror, 'you think they will try you—they will condemn you to death?'

'To be sure,' he said. 'But no matter; your courage has saved me in my own eyes, and my children's. For the world's opinion I care not one jot.'

Madcap neither moved nor spoke; every sense and faculty for the moment failed her, save that of seeing her father's body sharply outlined against a clear morning sky . . . and was he by such violent disruption of life as *this* to meet her mother?

'Only they must be quick about it,' he went on abruptly; 'for though you did not know it, I have been ill. Since I met Frank in town, there has been a fever in my blood, and my strength must have burnt out soon. Who's there?' he cried, as the key turned in the lock and the door opened.

It was Doune who entered, and God knows what memories of his father's care and tenderness, what thoughts of despair at the whole piteous tragedy, crowded on his mind as he drew near, and looked down upon the man who sat erect, neither clinging to nor supporting the daughter, whose arms were around him.

'Father,' said the young man, 'forgive me! I was mad when I saw you last, and your only brave, dutiful child is *there*.'

Mr. Eyre looked up, and realized that here was another soul with which to reckon, and one that he had practically left out of his calculations (for Madcap's mother and Madcap had absorbed all his thoughts)—a soul as stubborn and hard, if not as guilty, as his own.

Over Madcap's bowed head their glances met. There was death in the one, and immovable despair in the other; but as surely as the son knew that his father would shortly escape the consequences of his sin, so did the father that his son's life was not merely scorched, but blighted, by his sin.

'So you cannot endure what a woman can,' said Mr. Eyre; '*she*' (he touched Madcap's hair) ' is stronger.'

'She has no weaker life entwined with hers,' said Doune, a bitter ring in his hitherto lifeless voice; 'so that the hand that crushes one crushes both.'

'You mean Nancy?' said Mr. Eyre; 'well, she loves you, and you love her. If my crime keeps her from you, she is well lost.'

'Father,' said the young man, 'would you have married my mother, had you known that yours was to be the hand to end her life?'

'Ay, that would I!'

'And *I* would rather kill myself in cold blood!' exclaimed Doune, his eye kindling, and indignation breaking up the despairing calm of his features.

'Would that help her?' said Mr. Eyre; 'or, putting such a desperate remedy aside, think you a life lived apart from you, a slow death in which she looks and longs always for sign or sound of you—a death, in short, of *starvation*—is preferable to the one that you could give her? I have watched her,' he added abruptly: 'she is one of those who can love, and they are few. I never knew any others save——' he looked at Madcap, who had risen, and was standing by her brother's side.

'It is all over now, sir,' said Doune; 'I wrote to her this morning.'

For a brief moment father and son

seemed to change places. It was the former who looked beaten down, conquered of fate; Doune who stood erect and defied it. But even as the shield of a young girl's arms went round him, Mr. Eyre said, 'Leave us now, child;' and in a few moments the two men were alone together.

What passed between them was never known; but Doune at length came forth, pale indeed, but with such a look in his haggard eyes as told of hope springing once more in the heart that he had believed to be crushed beyond the power of either God or man to make whole again.

## CHAPTER XV.

'*Perchance and so thou purify thy soul,
And so thou lean on our fair father, Christ,
Hereafter in that world where all are pure,
We two may meet before High God, and thou
Wilt spring to me, and claim me thine.*'

IT was not Mr. Eyre's lot to be brought before any earthly tribunal more terrible than his own heart and his children's eyes, for in a very few days he had answered to a higher one, at which perhaps his only possible accuser, the one who had loved him best, would not appear.

He had got his death-blow in the moment that he discovered his guilt, and not even his daughter's devoted love could save him; the springs of life seeming to fail him suddenly, as though, with the death of his self-respect and honour, he too must cease to exist.

There had been no pretence even of his trial, and one day he was carried back to the Red Hall, where he lay till he died, with his children and Frank constantly beside him.

In those few short days the heart of the proud man at last found its Maker, and one of the truest signs of his repentance was when he sent for Hester, and asked her to forgive him.

As her burning tears fell on the hand she kissed, knowing how she had wronged and misunderstood him, her awful repentance for her sin outweighed his, and in the last look, the last words, for the first time these two erring souls understood one another.

His brain was perfectly clear, and he set his estate in order, and destroyed old letters, but gave into his daughter's hand a little packet that he desired her to bury with him. They were his sweetheart's love-letters—the only sweetheart of his life; and then he seemed to give himself no more concern about business, but went one afternoon to the bed whence he did not rise again.

That night he spoke of his little son Dody, who had died within a few days of his mother, and slept sound and sweet these seventeen years and more in her arms.

'I shall see him soon,' he said. 'I wonder if he will remember that I was unkind to him. Perhaps she has taught him to forgive me; and you always loved him, Frank, and he you. I've never asked *your* forgiveness, though I think *she* has; and I've left you another Madcap, my good, faithful child . . .'

He sank into a slumber even as he spoke, and did not wake till morning; then opened his eyes suddenly to see the three who stood beside him.

'*Light*,' he said; 'what is that verse of yours, child, I have so often heard you sing? So many things seem to have sunk into my soul lately, without my knowledge . . .'

Madcap drew in her breath hard as she repeated the words; but as she came to

'*Those angel faces I have lost erewhile,*'

across Mr. Eyre's face flashed a look of light—ay, and more light . . . perchance enough to guide his soul to his lost Madcap, as, stretching out his arms to his children, he passed away to that last tribunal where, by the grace of God, he may have found forgiveness for his sins.

THE END.

BILLING AND SONS, PRINTERS, GUILDFORD.

www.ingramcontent.com/pod-product-compliance
Lightning Source LLC
Chambersburg PA
CBHW032143230426
43672CB00011B/2433